Berlitz®

New York City

Original ...
Updated ... ...ovak
Principal p... ... Anna Mockford
and Nick Bonnetti
Cover photograph by Nick Bonnetti
Layout concept: Klaus Geisler
Picture Editor: Hilary Genin
Managing Editor: Tony Halliday

Berlitz® POCKET GUIDE
New York City

Sixth Edition (updated) 2004

Additional photography by:
Jay Fechtman (37, 39, 45, 74, 95, 98); Jon Davison (100, 102)

CONTACTING THE EDITORS

Every effort has been made to provide accurate information in this publication, but changes are inevitable. The publisher cannot be responsible for any resulting loss, inconvenience or injury. We would appreciate it if readers would call our attention to any errors or outdated information by contacting Berlitz Publishing, PO Box 7910, London SE1 1WE, England.
Fax: (44) 20 7403 0290;
e-mail: berlitz@apaguide.co.uk
www.berlitzpublishing.com

Holbein's *Sir Thomas More* is just one among a fine collection of mainly European paintings in the Frick Collection (page 48)

There is nothing more scenic or interesting than a stroll across the Brooklyn Bridge (page 30)

The Statue of Liberty (page 25) has welcomed millions to New York

TOP TEN ATTRACTIONS

The American Museum of Natural History (page 61) has some startling attractions ▼

◄ Washington Square Park lies at the heart of laid-back Greenwich Village (page 73)

After the destruction of the Twin Towers, the Empire State Building (page 45) once again has New York's highest observation deck ▶

The Lincoln Center for Performing Arts (page 59) is an important venue for opera and theater goers ▼

The Guggenheim (page 53) is known as much for its fine architecture as it is for its paintings ▶

The Met (page 50) has treasures from from every period of history ▶

Central Park (page 54) is New York's playground, with a huge variety of recreational activities ▶

CONTENTS

A ➤ in the text denotes a highly recommended sight

INTRODUCTION

First-time visitors to New York usually come with wide eyes and high expectations. And the city generally does not disappoint, even if it frustrates. Few places in the US are as entertaining as New York. No matter what it is you're after, you'll find it: great theater, marvelous museums, luxurious hotels, fascinating history, exciting nightlife, sumptuous dining. The only thing that might be difficult to find here is peace and quiet. But if you stay in a high-rise hotel far above the teeming streets, or venture into the upper reaches of Central Park, or walk out onto the terrace overlooking the Hudson River at the Cloisters, you can find some of that, too.

At first it can all be a little overwhelming: 12,000 taxis, almost 5,000 city buses, 6,400 miles of streets, 578 miles of waterfront, 21,000 restaurants, and 65,000 hotel rooms. However, once you get over the crowded streets, the wailing sirens, the multitude of hawkers, you can start to see that there is more to New York than its tourist attractions and museums. It's a place where people live. Sit on a bench in one of New York's 1,500 parks and watch them go by, or take a stroll through the maze of picturesque Greenwich Village streets.

> New Yorkers tend to refer to Manhattan as 'the city', even as they identify the other boroughs by name. For addresses, 'New York, New York' means Manhattan.

A City Transformed

If anything characterizes New York today, it's how much the city has raised itself up from the darker days of the 1970s

Vegetable stand in Lower Manhattan

and 1980s. Crime is now at levels New Yorkers have not seen since the 1960s, and the city is generally cleaner and more efficient than it has been for quite a while. As a result, both tourists and business people are flocking here in numbers not seen for years (though there was a perceptible – if only temporary – downturn in room reservations after the appalling events of September 11, 2001). Alongside the flourishing hotel trade, good new (and sometimes not very expensive) restaurants are also opening up right and left, which is great news for visitors and residents alike.

If you want to see an example of how the city can reinvent itself, just look at Times Square. A few years ago, the 'square' was filled with pornographic theaters, adult bookstores, and abandoned buildings. The Port Authority bus terminal was filled with hustlers and touts, and 42nd Street was really not a place one wanted to be after dark. Today Times Square is still choked, but with new, high-profile office buildings and hotels, refurbished Broadway theaters, shiny entertainment complexes, and tens of thousands of tourists. The adult theaters and bookstores have been banished for the most part, and media giants like MTV and Conde Nast have reclaimed the space along with stores like Toys R

The 9/11 Effect

Every American over a certain age can tell you the story of where they were and what they were doing when President John Kennedy was assassinated on November 22, 1963. Now, every New Yorker can tell you where they were and what they were doing the morning of September 11, 2001 when two terrorist-hijacked planes hit the World Trade Center. The average New Yorker has emerged from the tragedy of 9/11 feeling no less rushed and impatient about day-to-day life, but certainly less invincible and far more vulnerable.

Yellow cabs are part of New York's street furniture

Us and well-attended attractions like Madame Tussaud's Wax Museum. Some New Yorkers lament that Times Square is now just one big theme park, but the truth is that the area has never been more vibrant.

Not that the story is uniformly positive. The New York area has some of the highest unemployment and poverty rates in the country. The disparity between the rich (who are quite rich indeed) and the poor is greater than ever. Most of the new housing being built in the city will be affordable only to those with the highest incomes. Nevertheless, almost every New York neighborhood, from the South Bronx to Washington Heights, from the upscale Upper East Side to Jackson Heights in Queens, has a good story to tell.

A Heady Mix

It's difficult for mere mortals to live in such a complicated, crowded, and expensive city, so people can easily lose their tempers. But for a place as large and diverse as New York City undoubtedly is, everyone gets along pretty well. The five boroughs – Manhattan, Brooklyn, Queens, the Bronx, and Staten Island – have a total population of approximately 8 million. Brooklyn is the most populous, and Brooklyn and Queens each have more residents than Manhattan. There are more Italians than in Venice, more Irish than in Dublin, and more Jews than in Jerusalem. David Dinkins, a former mayor, was fond of calling New York a 'gorgeous mosaic.'

As a hub for immigration since colonial days, New York has always welcomed the world to sit at its table. Today they still arrive in large numbers, searching for wealth, or happiness, or freedom, or just a job; they come with an entrepreneurial spirit and perhaps nothing else. But they make the mixture richer, by bringing their language and traditions, their likes and dislikes. New York may not be a melting pot, but it is definitely a heady mix.

By the end of their first trip to New York, most visitors are hooked. Nothing is quite as exhilarating as walking the crowded streets of Midtown for the first time, or encountering works of art you've only read about in books, or seeing the Statue of Liberty looming over you from the ferry dock. Or even just strolling through Central Park on a blustery winter afternoon. Whatever you do, don't be intimidated. Walk purposefully, and you'll fit in just fine. Beneath their protective mantle, New Yorkers can sometimes feel just as overwhelmed as tourists. But you'd never know it by looking at them.

Rooftop art at the Met

A BRIEF HISTORY

Giovanni da Verrazano, a Florentine in the service of France, discovered what is now called New York Harbor in 1524, but it would be a hundred years before the first settlers came to the area. Today the entrance to the harbor (called the Verrazano Narrows) and the bridge across it are named after him.

New Amsterdam

In 1609, after the Englishman Henry Hudson, working for the Dutch East India Company, sailed up what is now the Hudson River to Albany, excitement finally began to build over the region's possibilities, and in 1624, the new Dutch West India Company sent the first settlers to what is now Lower Manhattan. The following spring the colonists built a small town at the site, calling it New Amsterdam. The first two Dutch governors of the territory, Peter Minuit and Peter Stuyvesant, oversaw the development of a lively trading post. According to a popular city creation myth, it was Peter Minuit who in 1626 purchased the entire island of Manhattan from Native Americans for the equivalent of $24 in beads and cloth, at the site of present-day Bowling Green.

From the beginning, New Amsterdam was the most cosmopolitan center in the New World. The earliest immigrants included Walloons, Scandinavians, Germans, Spaniards, and Portuguese Jews, not to mention black slaves from the Caribbean. In 1643 a priest counted 18 languages spoken in this town of 1,500 inhabitants. An atmosphere of religious tolerance even attracted British dissidents from New England.

In 1653 Governor Peter Stuyvesant built a wall across the expanse of the island – at present-day Wall Street – in an effort to protect the Dutch settlers from the British, who had

Detail from painting of George Washington returning to New York

settled much of the area around New Amsterdam. As it turned out, however, the effort was unnecessary. Unable or unwilling to put up a fight, the Dutch settlers surrendered to an English fleet on September 8, 1664. King Charles II gave the colony to his brother, the Duke of York, and New Amsterdam was rechristened New York.

New York

Although the city again came under Dutch control in 1673 (again without a fight) and was briefly known as New Orange, a treaty the following year returned it to British control. In the 18th century the town grew into a city of 25,000 and life became more comfortable. A city hall and several churches were built, and New York saw the foundation of King's College (today's Columbia University) as well as the creation of its first newspaper, but little of this era remains today. St. Paul's Chapel, built in 1766, is the oldest remaining church in New York. The Morris-Jumel mansion in Harlem also dates from this time.

British control of the colony of New York was a mixed success. Anti-British sentiment started early. In 1735 John Peter Zenger, publisher of the anti-government *New-York Weekly Journal*, was acquitted on charges of slander, an early victory for freedom of the press. (You can read more about the history of this victory at Federal Hall National Memorial in Lower Manhattan.) But the city was split between loyalists to the crown and pro-independence 'patriots.' On June 27, 1775 half the town went to cheer George Washington as he left to take command of the Continental Army in Boston, while the other half were down at the harbor giving a rousing welcome to the English governor, who had just returned from London. Similarly, the New York delegates voted against an early version of the Declaration of Independence.

The New Republic

New York remained a British stronghold throughout the Revolutionary War and only gave up after the final surrender in Virginia in 1781. Two years later England recognized the independence of the American colonies. Washington returned triumphantly to New York and bade farewell to his officers at Fraunces Tavern. He later became the country's first president, when the city was briefly the first capital of the new United States of America. Washington took the oath of office on the balcony of the original Federal Hall (formerly the New York City Hall), then went to pray at St. Paul's Chapel, where you can see his pew.

Although Philadelphia took over as the nation's political capital in 1790, New York remained America's commercial center. In 1800 (the same year Alexander Hamilton built the Grange, which is in today's Harlem), the population had reached 60,000 – twice what it had been ten years earlier.

> Many of New York's parks were originally potter's fields for the burial of the indigent. Both Bryant Park and Washington Square Park started out with this function.

The city was soon beset with housing shortages and sanitation problems. In the heat of summer, when disease and epidemics were commonplace, the inhabitants would escape to their 'country' homes in such far-flung places as the village of Greenwich (now Greenwich Village) or the wilderness that became today's Upper East Side. In 1811 the state legislature came to the conclusion that any further growth of New York City must be regulated. The Randel Commission proposed that all new streets should only cross each other at right angles, with streets running east–west and avenues north–south. (Broadway, already an established road leading to the north-west, was exempted.) The plan was immediately adopted, and as a result, everything above 14th Street is now a grid.

Burgeoning Town

When the Erie Canal opened in 1825, linking the Great Lakes to the Hudson River, New York became the ocean gateway for an immense hinterland. Business flourished and shipyards abounded in this major port; housing was still substandard, however, and most residents lived in crowded conditions. In December 1835 a fire destroyed the heart of the business district around Hanover and Pearl streets, including almost all that remained from the Dutch era. But the city recovered quickly from this calamity.

In 1853 the Crystal Palace of the first American World's Fair went up in present-day Bryant Park (behind the New York Public Library). That same year, the state legislature authorized the building of a great public space, Central Park; the architects, Calvert Vaux and Frederick Law Olmstead, were chosen five years later, the same year the Crystal Palace was destroyed by fire.

By 1860, the city's population had reached an unruly 800,000. Governing the city proved difficult, riots occasionally erupted, and, in general, crime was becoming a big problem. Rampant corruption in government was also taking its toll. William Marcy Tweed, who along with his cohorts in the Tammany Hall political organization ran New York City, managed to fleece the city of some $200 million. When 'Boss Tweed' was finally arrested in 1871, the city was in very bad shape indeed.

New York nevertheless once again proved its resilience and bounced back. The late 19th century and early 20th witnessed the city's most dramatic growth to date. Many of New York's existing magnificent buildings were built during this time. The construction of the railways that opened up the western lands, the expansion of mines and mills, and the development of the new petroleum and automobile industries were all financed by New York banks. Huge fortunes were made by the Vanderbilts, the Morgans, Carnegies, Rockefellers, and Fricks, among others. These tycoons amassed fabulous art collections and funded many of the philanthropic

Late 19th-century immigrants

and cultural institutions that make New York what it is today, from the Metropolitan Museum and Metropolitan Opera to the Frick Collection and the Rockefeller Center.

Mass Immigration

During the second half of the 19th century influxes of immigrants crowded into New York in search of a new and better life. The potato famine in Ireland and revolutionary ferment in Central Europe brought the Irish and Germans, who were soon followed by Italians, Poles, and Hungarians. The first

Skyscrapers

By the turn of the 20th century, the development of 'steel skeleton' construction made it possible to build tall. The first genuine skyscraper in New York was the **Flatiron Building**, erected in 1902 and relatively restrained with only 22 stories. The **Equitable Building**, however, which appeared on Lower Broadway in 1916, was a monster on an 'H'-shaped ground plan, with 40 floors, and filling an entire block. The walls were perpendicular, without any tiering, and thus the whole neighborhood was plunged into shadow. The city was compelled to pass a 'zoning law,' which stipulated that the upper floors of a skyscraper should be tiered to allow light through to the streets below. This resulted in the so-called 'wedding-cake' style of building, examples of which include the **Chrysler** and **Empire State Buildings** (1930 and 1931). Designed by Mies van der Rohe and Philip Johnson, and completed in 1958, the **Seagram Building** on Park Avenue was a simple tower with a straight facade, following the rules of the International Style. It overcame the zoning law by having a plaza at its base, setting the trend for later developments such as Rockefeller Center.

If you want to find out more about New York's skyscrapers, visit the **Skyscraper Museum** housed within the Ritz-Carlton Hotel development in Battery Park.

important wave of Jews fleeing the pogroms of Russia and Eastern Europe arrived in the 1880s. Over 2 million newcomers landed in the city between 1885 and 1895, welcomed (after 1886) by the Statue of Liberty.

While the middle class moved to west-side neighborhoods near Central Park, the comfortable brownstone houses and mansions of the rich spread up Fifth Avenue and onto the east side. In 1870, construction started on a bridge to connect New York City with Brooklyn, a sizeable city in its own right. The invention of the elevator by Elisha Otis made it

The Flatiron Building

possible to construct 'skyscrapers' up to the amazing height of eight or ten stories.

In 1898, New York City (from then on known as Manhattan), Brooklyn, Queens, the Bronx, and Staten Island merged to form Greater New York, with a population of more than 3 million. After London, Greater New York was the most populous city on earth.

The early years of the 20th century witnessed further impressive growth. Genuine skyscrapers – including the Flatiron Building (1902) – were built, the first subway line opened (1904), and Manhattan and Brooklyn were finally linked by an under-river subway tunnel (1908). When the business boom finally burst in 1929, bread lines and jobless people became a common sight; a shantytown even sprang up in Central Park. In 1934 a dynamic Italian-born mayor named Fiorello La Guardia fought to introduce an important number of public-welfare measures and civic reform initiatives, which have characterized the city ever since.

Highs and Lows

After World War II, the United Nations set up its headquarters in New York (on land donated by the Rockefeller family). The 1950s saw phenomenal growth in the city but also economic downturn. New highways and cheaper cars and houses encouraged city-dwellers to move to the suburbs. At the same time, in part because of this retreat, portions of the inner city began to decline. Even the beloved Brooklyn Dodgers moved to Los Angeles in 1958. True, Lincoln Center was developed and built in the 1960s, and the World's Fair was held in Flushing Meadows, Queens, in 1964–65, but racial tensions also led to riots in Harlem, Bedford-Stuyvesant, and the South Bronx. The city reached a low point in 1975 when New York teetered on the edge of bankruptcy.

After mixed fortunes in the 1980s, the 1990s brought better times. Things started looking up during the mayoralty of David Dinkins, the city's first black mayor, elected in 1989. But most of the improvements were not seen until the voting in of tart-tongued Rudolph Giuliani in 1993. A Republican mayor in a decidedly Democratic city, he brought order to the streets and cleaned up the grime. His 8-year term also accomplished such improvements as a planned subway line on Second Avenue in Manhattan and a rail link to Kennedy Airport in Queens. On 9/11, 2001 and its immediate aftermath, Mayor Giuliani took on the unexpected role as the very public face of a city in turmoil. He was succeeded in January 2002 by Mayor Michael Bloomberg, owner of the financial media empire that bears his name.

Historical Landmarks

1609 Englishman Henry Hudson is the first European to step on to the island known to the local Algonquin Indians as Mannahatta.

1624 The Dutch West India Company establishes a settlement on the southern tip of Mannahatta (now Battery Park), calling it New Amsterdam.

1664 War between England and Holland. New Amsterdam surrenders and is renamed New York after Charles II's brother, James, Duke of York.

1776 The Revolutionary War begins; the colonies declare independence. British troops occupy New York until 1783.

1785–90 New York is capital of the new United States of America.

1790 The first official census: New York has a population of 33,000.

1830 Irish and German immigrants begin arriving in great numbers.

1835 Part of Manhattan is ravaged by the 'Great Fire.'

1848–9 Political refugees arrive after failure of the German Revolution.

1857 William Marcy 'Boss' Tweed, elected to the County Board of Supervisors, launches a career of corruption. He eventually dies in jail.

1861–5 American Civil War. New York is on the winning, Yankee side.

1865 Italians, Jews, and Chinese begin arriving in large numbers.

1886 Statue of Liberty, a gift from France, is unveiled.

1892 Ellis Island becomes the entry point for imnlgrants.

1929 The Wall Street Crash, and the start of the Great Depression.

1931 The Empire State Building opens.

1933–45 Europeans take refuge in New York from Nazi persecution.

1941 The US enters World War II.

1946 The United Nations begins meeting in New York.

1973 The World Trade Center opens, the world's tallest building at the time.

1975 The city avoids bankruptcy via a loan from federal government.

1990 David Dinkins becomes the city's first African-American mayor.

1993 Rudolph Giuliani voted in as mayor and gets 'tough on crime.'

2000 Crowds flock to revitalized Times Square to see in the Millennium.

2001 Terrorists crash two hijacked passenger planes into the Twin Towers of the World Trade Center. The buildings collapse, killing close to 3,000 people.

2002 Tycoon Michael Bloomberg is sworn in as mayor.

WHERE TO GO

While the majority of visitors to New York never leave Manhattan, where most of the city's attractions are located, there is more to New York City than its most famous borough. Those who venture to Brooklyn will find a respectable art museum along with parks, gardens, and ethnic neighborhoods worth exploring. One of the country's great zoos is in the Bronx, near an equally notable attraction, the New York Botanical Garden. In Queens you'll find a topnotch film-making museum. Just getting to Staten Island requires an enjoyable ferry ride right by the Statue of Liberty, and best of all, it's free.

But it's Manhattan that draws the majority of visitors' attentions. Only 13½ miles (22km) long and 2 miles (3km) wide, New York's most popular borough is what everyone (including New Yorkers) calls 'the city.' So that's where we begin.

LOWER MANHATTAN

The oldest, most historic part of Manhattan is the Financial District at the tip of the island, roughly the area south of Worth Street, which begins just below Chinatown. Here you'll find Wall Street, the former site of the World Trade Center, South Street Seaport, and the ferries to Staten Island and the Statue of Liberty. After years of neglect, clubs and bars moved in, making the area worth a visit even after 7pm.

Ground Zero

For decades, the most visible tourist attraction in Lower Manhattan was the towering **World Trade Center** with its huge complex of offices, a hotel, shopping malls, subway

Manhattan from the Empire State Building

stations and the twin towers themselves, crowned by the Windows on the World restaurant and an Observation Deck. When the towers were opened in 1970, they were the tallest buildings in the world.

After the events of September 11, 2001 – when the towers became the target of terrorists causing the deaths of thousands of people from around the world and plunging the US into a state of alert for war – the site of the World Trade Center became a moving memorial, holding as much if not more meaning for visitors as when they came to marvel at its lofty peaks. Today, for many people, a tour of Lower Manhattan starts at what is called **Ground Zero**, the 16-acre (6-hectare) hole in the ground where the World Trade Center complex (actually a collection of seven buildings) once stood. New Yorkers and tourists alike can see for themselves what is left. What they find on the streets and sidewalks surrounding Ground Zero are tributes, signs and shrines left by other visitors who continue to stream into the area each day.

But New Yorkers, particularly those who live downtown, are ready to move on. The renowned architect Daniel Libeskind has been chosen to develop the site, but what will finally be built is very much a design in progress. It will be a commercial skyscaper incorporating a memorial.

Icon of Hope

Remarkable as it might seem, a huge globe-shaped metal sculpture, *The Sphere* by Fritz Koenig, which stood for more than 30 years in the World Trade Center Plaza, survived the tons of metal and concrete that crashed down upon it on 9/11. In March 2002, it was moved to nearby Battery Park where it is titled *An Icon of Hope*, standing at the foot of a bed of roses called Hope Garden. On the first anniversary of the attack, an eternal flame was lit here, in memory of the victims.

For a definitive update on the latest developments in Lower Manhattan, a good source of information is the Alliance for Downtown New York, Inc. From streetscapes to events of interest, almost everything worth knowing is on their website at <www.downtownny.com>.

9/11 survivor: the Icon of Hope in Battery Park

Battery Park City

When the World Trade Center was being built in the late 1960s, some 30 million tons of excavated landfill were dumped on adjoining Hudson River docks to create the site of what became, in the 1980s, **Battery Park City**, a collection of high- and low-rise apartment and office buildings and parks. A lovely esplanade – a favorite of in-line skaters and joggers – goes along the river all the way from the World Financial Center south to Battery Park City itself.

The highlight of the **World Financial Center** is the fine **Winter Garden**, a public atrium ringed by shops, restaurants, and bars. Grab a take-out from a cafe and join the stockbrokers on one of the benches, or enjoy a more upscale lunch at one of the sit-down restaurants. Outside on the docks, you can take the New York Waterway Colgate Ferry to New Jersey (every 15 minutes) to connect to a bus for the **Liberty Science Center** (daily 9.30am–5.30pm; admission fee), which, though not strictly a New York City attraction, is a fun place to explore with its range of interactive exhibits.

A stroll (or skate) down the promenade is a pleasant way to spend an hour, and also a great place to view the sunset. At the end of the promenade, near the Bowling Green subway station, you'll find the **Museum of Jewish Heritage** (Sun–Wed 9am–5pm, Thur 9am–8pm, Fri 9am–2pm, closed Sat and Jewish holidays; admission fee). Described as a 'Living Memorial to the Holocaust,' it's actually quite a bit more. Beyond the first floor's interesting multimedia introductory show are galleries about Jewish life and culture; the second floor is devoted to the Holocaust, while the third floor is devoted to exhibits about Judaism today. By focusing on the complexity of Jewish life in the 20th century, the museum is much less depressing than others devoted solely to the Holocaust.

Battery Park City

Nearby is **Battery Park**, a leafy expanse at the tip of Manhattan. If you watch the crowds, you'll notice that most of them are heading for **Castle Clinton**, which has played many roles in New York's history. Originally the South-west Battery, a fortification to help protect ships in New York from the English navy, the building dates to 1811. By 1824, its military mission fulfilled, the fort became a concert hall, immigration check-point, and even for a while the site of the New York City Aquarium. The National Park Service took over the building in the late 1940s and renamed it Castle Clinton. It was re-opened in 1975 as the site of a small museum and as the ticket office for ferries to the Statue of Liberty and Ellis Island *(see below)*.

Looming over the square is the **Old Customs House**, now the home of the **National Museum of the American Indian** (daily 10am–5pm, Thur to 8pm; free), a branch of the Smithsonian Institution in Washington, DC (the other Smithsonian branch in NYC is the Cooper-Hewitt on the Upper East Side). The museum celebrates native American culture and showcases a variety of artifacts. There are also films shown on the premises, plus a very nice gift shop, and (for researchers), an impressive archive of information.

Across from Battery Park's northern tip, at the foot of Broadway, is a triangular patch called Bowling Green. It is said that this is where Peter Minuit bought Manhattan from Native Americans for $24 in 1626. Today it is the site of one New York's many Greenmarkets, selling fresh local produce (Tues and Thur 8am–5pm).

Statue of Liberty and Ellis Island

Ferries for the Statue of Liberty and Ellis Island leave from the **South Ferry** dock, calling first at the Statue of Liberty (daily between 8.30am and 4.30pm in summer, departures every 20 minutes; between 9am and 3.45pm in winter, departures every 45 minutes).

The **Statue of Liberty** is the most recognized icon of New York City, perhaps of the United States. Some ten years in the making, it was a gift from France in recognition of the friendship between the two countries and has served as a beacon for immigrants arriving in the New World for over 100 years.

Ferry to the Statue of Liberty

Creator Frédéric-Auguste Bartholdi's 151-ft- (46-meter-) high structure is one of those wild dreams that become reality. Engineering expertise had to be harnessed to art, so Bartholdi called in Gustave Eiffel – yes, that Eiffel – to help translate his vision into metal. Parisian workmen erected the statue in 1884, as bemused Parisians watched her crowned head rise above their rooftops. It was later dismantled and shipped in 214 huge wooden crates for re-assembly on Liberty Island. The statue of *Liberty Enlightening the World* was unveiled by President Cleveland on October 28, 1886 and received a major overhaul and cleaning for a grand re-opening in 1986.

Once you arrive on Liberty Island, head for the elevator to the promenade at the top of the 89-ft- (27-meter-) high base of the statue. You should expect at least an hour's wait, but the views of Manhattan are superb, much better in fact than the view from the crown. In order to reach the lady's crown, you'll have to climb a 22-story staircase. At the time of going to press, however, the statue was still closed for security reasons (tel: 212-363-3200 for the latest access information). If you don't make the climb, there is a museum in the base, and you are free to walk around the island.

After the statue, the ferry continues to **Ellis Island**. The island itself was created mostly from landfill from the building of the New York subway system. The museum, which opened in 1990, retraces, through film, audio-visual displays, and permanent and changing exhibitions, the sufferings and joys of some 12 million immigrants who entered the United States through these doors between 1892 and 1924, when consulates abroad took over the screening process. You might find a long lost family member on the Immigrant Wall of Honor. Among notable personalities who made it through Ellis Island were actors Claudette Colbert, Bob Hope, and Edward G. Robinson, composer Irving Berlin, the Von Trapp family of *The Sound of Music* fame, and poet Khalil Gibran.

Staten Island Ferry

If you're itching to get back out to sea, another ferry ride is available from the tip of Manhattan, at the end of Battery Park – the Staten Island Ferry. There's not much of interest to visitors on Staten Island since New York's most distant borough is mostly residential, but the 20-minute ferry ride alone is well worth the trip. And best of all, it's free. You'll get stunning views of the Statue of Liberty and the Manhattan skyline receding in the distance, and since the ferry runs 24 hours a day, you can get the same view a night.

The Statue of Liberty

Fraunces Tavern

Near the ferry terminal, at 54 Pearl Street (at Broad Street) is **Fraunces Tavern**. First opened for business in 1762 (the original building

Fraunces Tavern

dated to 1719), this is where George Washington is said to have bid farewell to his officers after the Revolutionary War. The building you see today is mostly a recreation, built in 1907. Colonial history buffs may appreciate the modest museum upstairs (Tues, Wed, Fri and Sat 10am–5pm; Thurs 10am–7pm), which contains historical documents and period furniture, as well as items such as a lock of Washington's hair, a fragment of one of his teeth, and a shoe that belonged to his wife, Martha; others may opt to dine in the pseudo-colonial atmosphere of the restaurant downstairs together with banker and stockbrokers (weekdays only).

The immediate area is absolutely teeming with remnants of old New York. After leaving Fraunces Tavern, if you walk to the right on Pearl Street and turn left at the next corner, you'll come to **Stone Street**, another historic district with a colonial street plan and buildings that were formerly dry goods warehouses and stores. At the other end of Stone Street, after a quick jog to the right, you'll be back on Pearl Street and Hanover Square, which was a wealthy neighborhood during colonial days,

► Wall Street

If you continue on Pearl Street, after a couple of blocks you will come to **Wall Street**, perhaps one of the most famous streets in the world, if only for its metaphoric heft. (There was once an actual wall here, built in 1653 by Dutch governor Peter Stuyvesant to protect settlers of New Amsterdam from the British). Turn left on Wall Street to find several buildings of note. Number 55 Wall Street, which dates to 1842, is one of the oldest buildings on Wall Street; 40 Wall Street, formerly the Bank of Manhattan, is one of the tallest buildings in New York. If by this time you hadn't understood why people often refer to the 'canyons' of Lower Manhattan, the implications should be coming clear now; the skyscrapers here are closer together than any other place in the city.

At 26 Wall Street (at Nassau), you'll see a large statue of Washington outside **Federal Hall National Memorial**, formerly the US Customs building. The original building, demolished in 1812, was the home of the United States government for a year when New York was briefly the nation's capital; it's also where Washington took the oath as the first president of the US, on 30 April 1789. Inside is a modest museum, which is free (Mon–Fri 9am–5pm).

Reflections on Broad Street

Most visitors to the city are more interested in the building across the street, the **New York Stock Exchange**, at 8–18 Broad Street. Interestingly, though Wall Street is synonymous with stock trading, the building's entrance is on the cross street. The public gallery and visitors center have traditionally been open weekdays, its shiny allure making it one of New York's busiest attractions, complete with interactive machines and displays. Since the events of September 11, 2001, however, it is advisable to call the visitors center, tel: (212) 656-5165, to find out whether the gallery is currently open to the public.

Brooklyn Bridge

There are a few other sights of interest to visitors in Lower Manhattan. At the corner of Broadway and Fulton streets is **St Paul's Chapel** and its churchyard. George Washington worshiped here after his inauguration; you can see his pew on the right side of the church as you enter from the front.

A little farther up at 233 Broadway stands the **Woolworth Building**, which reigned as the world's tallest building from 1913 until the Chrysler Building ushered in the skyscraper age in 1930. You can't go upstairs, but take a look at the ornate lobby. Just up Broadway is **New York City Hall**, which is fairly unassuming. And if you're in the mood for a stroll, there is none more scenic or interesting than a trip by foot across the **Brooklyn Bridge**, which opened in 1833 (before then, the only way to Brooklyn was by ferry). The entrance to the pedestrian walkway is on the east side of City Hall Park; take a walk all the way to Brooklyn Heights.

The Brooklyn Bridge

One more detour may be in order for history buffs. At 241 Water Street is the **Seaman's Church Institute**, which has a gallery and ship models. But many are drawn to the area for what is across the street, the **Titanic Memorial Lighthouse**, erected in memory of those lost on the ill-fated ocean liner.

Historic vessels at South Street Seaport

South Street Seaport

A final area of interest in this part of Lower Manhattan is the **South Street Seaport**. This 11-acre (4-hectare), nine-block enclave on the East River at the foot of Fulton Street was once in the middle of the nation's busiest working docks. But its usefulness faded, and in the 1960s, the area was turned into a pedestrian mall. In addition to the **South Street Seaport Museum** (daily 10am–5pm, Thur until 8pm, closed Tues fall and spring; admission fee), which features mostly nautical memorabilia, there are half a dozen historic ships moored at **Pier 17**, which you can visit as a part of your museum admission fee. This is a popular spot for summer concerts, shopping, and dining.

The mall at Pier 17 has the usual collection of stores and mediocre restaurants. Bypass these unless you're in the mood for shopping, and head upstairs to see the great view of the Brooklyn Bridge. If you happen to be in the area around 4am, you can see the nearby **Fulton Fish Market** at its busiest. The wholesale market, an authentic survivor of the area as it once was, operates only at night, so it's pretty much deserted by 6am.

MIDTOWN – THE THEATER DISTRICT

➤ Times Square

Once a seedy, not-so-pleasant place to be, **Times Square** lies at the intersection of Broadway and Seventh Avenue, at the heart of Manhattan's theater district (roughly the area between 42nd and 53rd streets between Sixth and Eighth avenues). Back in the *Midnight Cowboy* years of the early 1970s, it had reached a distinct low point. For a time, the area may have been the 'crossroads of the world,' but it seemed to be so for only the down and out. Now, it has gotten a new lease on life. Gone are most of the hustlers and prostitutes and pornographic theaters and bookstores; in their place are smart new office buildings, hotels, stores, restaurants, and other attractions that appeal to New Yorkers and tourists alike. One can debate whether this change has

---

Broadway

The name Broadway today is synonymous with theaters, shows, musicals, entertainment, and the glitzy world of the Great White Way, as the section between 40th and 53rd streets was referred to after electric light made its appearance for the first time. Its heyday was in the 1920s and '30s, when there were over 80 theaters on and around Broadway. The most famous section was 42nd Street – so famous in fact that theater owners whose properties were actually on 41st or 43rd Street had passageways constructed through entire blocks of buildings just to be able to boast a 'Forty-Second Street' address.

made the area blander, but it certainly has revived it as the dynamic heart of Manhattan.

The 'square' is named for the *New York Times*, whose headquarters was once at 1 Times Square (where the ball drops on New Year's Eve). The *Times* has since moved west on 43rd Street to a much larger building, but the name stuck.

Look west down 42nd Street, and you can see some of the newly refurbished theaters and entertainment centers that are bringing new life to the area. On the north side of 42nd Street is the **New Victory Theater**,

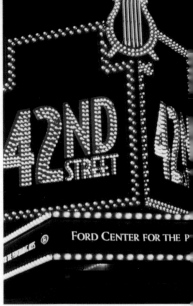

Broadway's most famous section

which specializes in children's productions; beyond the new **Ford Center for the Performing Arts** is the new **E-Walk** entertainment complex, which houses a 24-screen movie theater as well as other amusements. On the south side of 42nd Street is a **Madame Tussaud's Wax Museum**. On the northeast corner of 42nd and Broadway is the ESPN **Zone**, which has a theme restaurant as well as an amusement arcade.

Duffy Square

Across Broadway is **Duffy Square**, a patch of cement between Seventh Avenue and Broadway at 47th Street, which is the location for the TKTS discount theater ticket booth, where you can purchase half-price theater tickets for same-

Hot dog stalls are ubiquitous

day performances. There is another TKTS booth at the South Street Seaport *(see page 31)*.

If you stand in Duffy Square, you can see many of the newer landmarks of the area. Across the street in the Bertelsmann building (at 45th Street) is the **Virgin Megastore**, which tends to be jammed day and night. At the corner of 44th Street is the Viacom building where MTV's **Times Square Studio** is located. On the east side of Duffy Square (also at 44th Street), is the new corner studio for *Good Morning America*. All around are the hotels, restaurants, and amusements that have made the revived Times Square as popular as it's ever been.

Port Authority

West of Times Square, on 42nd Street at Eighth Avenue, is the **Port Authority of New York**, the city's main bus station. Once the scariest place in Manhattan, it's still not picturesque, but it is now a thriving and not unpleasant commuter hub, where you can get the bus without being descended on by scores of touts and hustlers.

On the far west side of Manhattan, at the very end of 46th Street, is the **Intrepid Sea-Air-Space Museum** (Tues–Sun 10am–5pm, Mon summer only; admission fee). The Intrepid, a decommissioned US Navy aircraft carrier, is packed with exhibits about sea exploration and warfare, space travel, and aviation. Two other major components of the museum are the submarine *USS Growler*, and the destroyer *USS Edison*. The museum is popular, though it's a little hard to get to (take the M 50 bus on 49th Street). A new visitor center is a plus.

North of Times Square at 1697 Broadway (53rd and 54th streets) is the **Ed Sullivan Theater**, where *Late Night with David Letterman* is based. NYC & Company operates a visitor center at 810 Seventh Avenue (52nd and 53rd streets). At 135 W. 55th Street (at 7th Ave.) is **City Center**. Once a Masonic hall, it is now a theater and dance complex. It's the home of Manhattan Theatre Club. Two blocks north is **Carnegie Hall** (154 W. 57th Street), one of New York's most famous performing

Financed by the iron and steel magnate Andrew Carnegie, Carnegie Hall was first opened in 1891. Now fully refurbished, it is one of the great music venues of the city, and one of the few to survive waves of development. If you can't make it to a concert here, at least have a look at the new museum.

arts spaces; the main concert hall is said to have the best acoustics in New York. Across the street is the tourist favorite, Hard Rock Café.

CENTRAL MIDTOWN

East of Times Square is another great New York restoration project of the early 1990s. At 42nd Street, between Sixth and Fifth avenues, are the green and leafy expanses of **Bryant Park**. The present French-style layout of the park dates from the Great Depression, but by the 1980s it had become a no-man's land of drug dealers night and day. Now it is one of midtown's most pleasant oases, where office workers gather

The New York Public Library

in the summer months for lunch or just to relax; frequent special events are held.

The park lies behind the **New York Public Library**, a Beaux-Arts-style building that dates to 1911; two very handsome, famous and much-photographed stone lions, Patience and Fortitude, flag its Fifth Avenue entrance. One of the largest research libraries in the world, the structure houses several million books, almost as many manuscripts, and vast reading rooms. The main reading room, which was re-opened in 1999 after a major restoration, has been modernized and brought back to its original grandeur. Changing exhibitions are regularly mounted in the library's exhibition halls.

West 47th is New York's **Diamond District**, an area dominated by mostly Orthodox Jewish diamond dealers; believe it or not, a majority of the diamonds that pass through New York find their way to this unassuming street. While this may be a good place to shop for diamonds, it's questionable as to whether or not you'll find any real bargains at the jewelry or discount electronics stores.

► Rockefeller Center

The centerpiece of central Manhattan, covering 22 acres (9 hectares) between Fifth and Sixth avenues, from 47th to 51st streets, is **Rockefeller Center**. All the buildings in this complex are linked by underground walkways and concourses, which are themselves filled with shops, a post office, and restaurants. Columbia University purchased the site in 1811 when it was still farmland. In 1928, John D. Rockefeller, a founder of the Standard Oil Company, asked the university for a lease on the site to raise a commercial complex. Built mostly between 1931 and 1940, Rockefeller Center attracts tens of thousands of office-workers, visitors, and shoppers daily. Much of the area, including the centerpiece ice-skating rink, has undergone major renovation.

From Fifth Avenue you enter via the **Channel Gardens**, a sloping walkway divided by fountains and flowerbeds between the British and French buildings, which end at the sunken plaza and its famous gilded **statue of Prometheus**. This is also where the giant Christmas tree is placed (right behind Prometheus). If you have time, wander around and admire some of the Art Deco details.

Nowadays, the **GE Building** (the largest building in the complex) is better known as the headquarters for the NBC

The famous statue of Prometheus at Rockefeller Center

Radio City Music Hall

television network and the *Today Show* – the glassed-in studio is across the street from the building's southeast corner (at 49th Street).

Also at this corner is the NBC **Experience**, a combination attraction and store for merchandise festooned with the logo of the network and some of its television shows. You can also buy tickets here for the NBC Studio Tour, whose high price doesn't seem to detract from its popularity; tours leave every 30 minutes from 8.30am to 5.30pm. The Rainbow Room, atop the GE Building, was a popular and magical supper club for several years but is now a private catering hall (with plans to open a small restaurant or bar).

Radio City Music Hall (at the corner of 6th Avenue and 50th Street) is one of the largest theaters in the world, with a seating capacity of around 6,000. This restored Art Deco masterpiece is the popular location for seasonal theme shows, including the dazzling Christmas Spectacular; it's of course also the home of the ever-popular Rockettes. Stage Door Tours can be arranged by calling (212) 247 4777.

EAST MIDTOWN

At the turn of the 20th century, Fifth Avenue was the location of one of the largest and most opulent mansions in New York. After World War I, a number of fashionable and expensive stores opened for business here. You'll still find Saks Fifth Avenue (50th Street), Henri Bendel (55th and 56th streets), Tiffany's (57th Street), and Bergdorf Goodman (57th Street), though most of the trendiest designers now have their boutiques on Madison Avenue. The gaudiest addition to Fifth Avenue has without a doubt been Donald Trump's **Trump Tower** (56th and 57th streets), where a 'wall' of water slides down rose marble set between gleaming brass escalator rails; in addition to the ritzy stores, you'll also find a Tower Records.

St Patrick's Cathedral, on Fifth Avenue (50th and 51st), was the tallest building in the vicinity when it was built between 1858 and 1874. Today, however, it appears somewhat dwarfed by the skyscrapers of Rockefeller Center and the apartment building next door, though the juxtaposition of its soft gray granite and the surrounding glass creates a stunning image. Seat of the Archdiocese of New York City, the church is the focal point of the Irish parade on St Patrick's Day.

St Patrick's Cathedral

Museum of Modern Art

One of midtown's most important cultural centers is the **Museum of Modern Art** (MOMA), on 53rd Street between Fifth and Sixth avenues. However, MOMA Manhattan is presently closed for renovation and extension work, and won't reopen until 2005. Meanwhile, the bulk of the collection has relocated to MOMA QNS, 33rd Street and Queens Boulevard in the borough of Queens. The MOMA Design Store, one

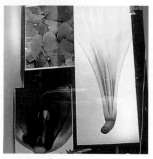

American Folk Art display

of the best places to buy artistically designed household-wares, remains open on West 53rd Street.

Devoted to works of art created after 1880, roughly from the Impressionists on, the MOMA collection includes such masterpieces as Van Gogh's *Starry Night*, Rousseau's *Sleeping Gypsy*, Wyeth's *Christina's World*, a number of Monet's *Water Lilies*, as well as important works of Picasso, Jackson Pollock, Mark Rothko, Chuck Close, and Salvador Dali. Modern sculpture is not ignored, and there are examples of everything from Marcel Duchamp's bicycle wheel as sculpture to huge installations by contemporary performance artists. The model of Frank Lloyd Wright's *Falling Water* is a popular exhibit, the study of architecture as an art form being one of the museum's great strengths (as is its photography).

Due west of the temporarily closed MOMA, at 45 West 53rd Street, is the new **American Folk Art Museum** (Tues–Sun 10am–6pm, Fri to 8pm; admission fee). Celebrating the 'extraordinary accomplishments of ordinary people,' the museum has exhibits ranging from 18th- and 19th-century paintings, to quilts, to contemporary sculpture.

Across 53rd Street is the **Museum of Arts and Design** (Tues–Sun 10am–6pm, Thurs to 8pm; admission fee) and its interesting collection of everything from teapots to antique quilts, old-fashioned rocking chairs to contemporary Native American pottery.

At the corner of Fifth Avenue and 59th Street, busy **Grand Army Plaza** marks the division between Fifth Avenue's shopping area and the residential section, which is lined with exclusive apartment buildings and a few remaining mansions. This is the place to hire a horse-drawn carriage for a ride round Central Park *(see page 54)*. It's also the site of two of New York's most famous hotels, the **Plaza** and the **Pierre** (at East 61st Street). Across from the plaza, set a little way back from the avenue, is the General Motors Building and the giant toy store, **F.A.O. Schwarz** (where you can still see the CBS *Early Show* studio being broadcast from a street-level studio).

The International Center of Photography at 1133 Avenue of the Americas at 43rd Street (Tues–Thurs 10am–5pm, Fri 10am–8pm, weekends 10am–6pm; admission fee) houses a collection of over 40,000 items covering the entire history of photography, in the heart of midtown.

Plaza Hotel entrance

The streets after 50 east of Fifth Avenue have several places of interest to visitors. The **Sony Wonder** technology lab in the Sony Building (formerly the AT&T Building) at 550 Madison Avenue (at 55th) is aimed at the younger set; parents can shop at Sony Style downstairs. The 57-story tower of the **New York Palace Hotel** (East 50th and 51st) incorporates the historic Villard Houses, which date to 1885. Take a walk through the grand lobby if you are in the area. The rest of the historic part of the hotel has been turned into Le Cirque 2000, a famously expensive restaurant.

A Park Avenue landmark is the **Waldorf-Astoria Hotel**, which takes up the entire block between Park and Lexington from 49th to 50th. It has been host to world leaders since 1931. Nearby are two other landmark office towers. The bronze-and-glass **Seagram Building**, on Park Avenue between 52nd and 53rd, is the only New York building designed by the great architect Mies van der Rohe; it's also the home of the famous Four Seasons restaurant (52nd Street).

► Grand Central

After a long renovation, **Grand Central Terminal** (at 42nd between Park and Lexington) has been returned to its former splendor. Completed in 1913, the building itself is a great Beaux-Arts masterpiece. Inside, 31 rail lines arrive on the upper level, 17 on the lower. The central concourse, vast but also light, airy, and harmonious under a blue-green, star-sprinkled ceiling 12 stories high, is invaded every afternoon from 4 to 6 by hundreds of thousands of suburban commuters catching their trains home to points north of Manhattan. If you enter from the Vanderbilt Avenue side of the station, look directly across the lobby to see the grand staircase, which was only recently added to the building. New restaurants have opened, and the terminal hallways on the Lexington Avenue and 42nd Street sides are now filled

Grand Central sculpture

with upscale shops. And of course, one cannot forget the famous **Oyster Bar & Restaurant** on the lower level, still a favorite for area power-lunchers. Free tours are offered twice a week, every Wednesday at 12.30pm by the Municipal Arts Society (meet at the information booth on the Grand Concourse; tel: 212-935 3960), and every Friday by the Grand Central Partnership (meet in front of the Whitney Museum at Philip Morris on 42nd Street; tel: 212-883 2420).

The Chrysler Building

The Whitney Museum of American Art at Altria is located just across 42nd Street, south of Grand Central at 120 Park Avenue. The small gallery, which is free, presents four exhibitions each year; adjoining is a much larger sculpture court, which also has a coffee bar. It's a good place to rest your feet.

Across Lexington Avenue on 42nd Street stands the most beautiful skyscraper of all, the **Chrysler Building**, a silvery Art-Deco needle completed in 1930. A recent cleaning has made the top of the building gleam; a major interior renovation should give it life through the next century. For a few months it was the tallest structure in the world, but it was rapidly surpassed by the Empire State Building *(see page 43)*. The stylized eagle heads on the upper corners were modeled on the Chrysler automobile's 1929 radiator cap.

Daily News décor

At the corner of Second Avenue, even more fine Art-Deco architecture distinguishes the former **Daily News Building**; the lobby, with its huge revolving dome is well worth a look. The paper moved west of Penn Station a few years ago. Also well worth a look is the **Ford Foundation** headquarters (320 East 42nd Street); offices open onto a spacious interior court with trees – New York's first office-building atrium. It's another of the city's fine public spaces.

▶ United Nations

The eastern end of 42nd Street used to be a warren of tenements and slaughterhouses, but thanks to John D. Rockefeller, Jr., it is now the home of the **United Nations**. A team of 11 architects, including Wallace K. Harrison, Le Corbusier, and Oscar Niemeyer, designed the buildings, which were completed in the early 1950s. The Secretariat is housed in the glass-and-marble upright structure, while the General Assembly meets in the lower building with the slightly concave roof. The flags of all the member nations flutter from the flagpoles along First Avenue.

When the General Assembly is not in session, visitors from around the world take daily multilingual tours of the General Assembly Hall and Council Chambers, the sculptures in the grounds overlooking the East River and Queens, and informative documentary exhibits. A highlight is the meditation room adorned with stained-glass windows by Marc Chagall.

SOUTH MIDTOWN

Empire State Building

Who knows the name of the tallest building in the world? Well, it's not the **Empire State Building** (corner of 5th Avenue and 34th Street, daily 9.30am–midnight; admission fee). Though it no longer holds the title, it is otherwise everything a skyscraper should be: 102 stories; 60,000 tons of steel; 3,500 miles (5,632 km) of telephone wires and cables; 60 miles (97 km) of pipes; a total volume of 1¼ million cubic yards (1 million cubic meters); 1,860 steps, and of course, its towering height – 1,414 ft (431 m), including the TV antenna (over all, half as tall again as the Eiffel Tower). Opened in 1931 in the depths of the Great Depression, the building took just two years to complete. The 86th-floor Observation Deck provides stunning views of New York. On the outside terrace you can see much of Manhattan, including Central Park, and on a clear day you can see ships 40 miles (64 km) out to sea. The intrepid can go up to the 102nd-floor observation deck, right up where King Kong swatted at wasp-like attacking airplanes, for a slightly better view.

The Empire State Building

Back on earth, you can go west along 34th Street to visit **Macy's** (6th and 7th

Taking in the view from the Empire State's observation deck

avenues), New York's most famous and largest department store, and also the Manhattan Mall. Nearby, at 7th Avenue and 33rd Street, is **Madison Square Garden**, renowned for boxing matches and rock concerts. In addition to being home to the New York Knicks (basketball) and the Rangers (ice hockey), it is also used as a conference center. The Garden seats 20,000 people and its adjacent theater can take an additional 5,000. Under Madison Square Garden is Pennsylvania Station (usually referred to as Penn Station), the railway terminal for New Jersey and Long Island commuters and for Amtrak. Across Eighth Avenue is the **General Post Office**, which was a twin to the old Penn Station, torn down in the late 1960s to make room for Madison Square Garden. The post office building is poised to become a new, even grander Penn Station in the near future.

If you are in New York for a trade show, chances are that you'll head for the **Jacob K. Javits Convention Center**, the city's largest exhibition center, a striking building on 11th Avenue between 34th and 37th streets. Designed by I.M. Pei, the center was named for New York state's long-time Republican senator.

To the east of the Empire State Building, at 36th and Madison in Murray Hill, is another prominent landmark: the **Morgan Library**. J. Pierpont Morgan's personal collection of rare books and manuscripts includes a Gutenberg Bible and Florentine sculpture and art. Often overlooked by tourists, it's a quiet place, which is one of its pleasures. However, it is closed for renovation until 2006.

UPPER EAST SIDE – THE MUSEUM MILE

Home to many of New York's famous museums, the Upper East Side starts at 59th Street, at the corner of Central Park. Beyond the east 60s, much of this area is residential, and includes some of the most expensive real estate in Manhattan. This is where you'll find the former residence of Jacqueline Onassis and the current residences of many of New York's society doyennes.

CityPass

One way to see several of Manhattan's top attractions and save some money is to buy a CityPass, which gives you admission to seven leading attractions (the Empire State Building Observation Deck, the Guggenheim Museum, The Museum of Modern Art, the Intrepid Sea-Air-Space Museum, the American Museum of Natural History, the Circle Line Harbor Cruise and the Whitney Museum of American Art), for only $45, considerably less than the total for individual full admission prices. You can buy the pass at any of the participating attractions; it can be used for nine consecutive days and enables you to avoid most ticket lines.

Most of the Upper East Side's museums are located along the so-called 'Museum Mile' from 82nd to 104th streets. But there are a few exceptions. One is the **Mount Vernon Hotel Museum and Gardens**, at 421 East 61st Street (1st and York avenues; open Tues–Sun 1–5pm; admission fee). This Federal-style house, which dates from 1799, is an interesting period piece for those with time and interest, featuring 19th-century furnishings and decorative arts.

▶ Frick Collection

A few other major museums are just off the Museum Mile proper. The **Frick Collection** at 70th Street and 5th Avenue (Tues–Sat 10am–6pm, Sun 1–6pm; admission fee) is situated in the former mansion of coal and steel baron Henry Clay Frick, who put together one of the finest private collections of art in the US (mostly European paintings and sculpture).

The Frick mansion and gardens

Upon the death of Frick's widow in 1931, their home, which was designed by Thomas Hastings, and the art therein were donated to the city of New York as a museum; it opened in 1935 after a reconstruction designed by John Russell Pope. Visitors to the collection have the extreme pleasure of seeing not only beautiful works of art but also the mansion and its gardens, much as they were when the Fricks lived there.

The attractive red-granite building on the northeast corner of Park Avenue and 70th Street is the headquarters of the Asia Society. The society mounts imaginative exhibitions of ancient and modern Asian and Pacific art assembled from private collections, as well as from its own permanent collection. It's open Tues–Sun 11am–6pm, Fri until 9pm.

And it's a rare and wonderful experience. In addition to three Vermeers (including *Mistress and Maid*), the museum holds fine works by Holbein *(Sir Thomas More and Thomas Cromwell)*, El Greco *(St Jerome)*, Bellini *(St Francis in Ecstasy)*, Boucher, Titian, Goya, Whistler, Rembrandt, and Velázquez; exquisite European furniture; and one of the largest collections of small bronze sculptures in the world.

Whitney Museum

Located on Madison Avenue (at 75th Street) is the excellent **Whitney Museum of American Art** (Tues, Wed, Fri–Sun 11am– 6pm, Thurs 1–8pm; admission fee), which is unique for several reasons. First of all, it was founded by an artist (Gertrude Vanderbilt Whitney), though admittedly an artist from one of New York's wealthiest families. Second, it is one of the few museums that is dedicated solely to American art and that seeks out works from alternative media (such as film and video). The Whitney seems to go out of its way to cause controversy with its spring Biennial exhibition. But by focusing its collection on contemporary American artists (both those of Ms. Whitney and those of today), it has also gone a long way toward changing attitudes about the diversity and strength of American art. The permanent collection includes interesting works from such artists as Andy Warhol, Alexander Calder, Georgia O'Keefe, Joseph Stella, Jackson Pollock, Jasper Johns, and Mark Rothko. Curators continue to build and show works by living artists. (A branch is also located at Whitney at Altria, Park Avenue and 42nd Street.)

▶ Metropolitan Museum of Art

Museum Mile begins at the **Metropolitan Museum of Art**, located at 82nd Street and 5th Avenue (Tues–Thurs, Sun 9.30am–5.15pm; Fri–Sat 9.30am–8.45pm; admission fee). Monumentally huge, the 'Met,' as it is affectionately known,

The Metropolitan Museum of Art

is a repository for all things cultural, from Egyptian mummies to Roman bronzes to Chinese pottery to wonderful Impressionist paintings. Founded in 1870, the institution owns over 3 million items, though only around a quarter of the total collection is on display at any one time in its nearly 250 rooms. The Greek and Roman galleries have been

Egyptian exhibit at the Met

recently renovated and are now airy and bright, a wonderful venue for some exquisite works that people often overlook on the way to the cafeteria; they are worth a closer look. Also recently refurbished are the galleries devoted to Chinese art. Children love the Egyptian galleries (the best such collection in the US), especially the Temple of Dendur, which sits in its own room with a view of Central Park. But they also enjoy the Arms and Armor halls and the African galleries.

Don't miss the American Wing, particularly the tranquil Garden Court. You'll find stained-glass windows, the facade of a Wall Street bank, fountains, and sculptures, along with plants and benches to sit on to quietly contemplate the surroundings. On all sides are period rooms and other galleries that show off the Met's fine holdings in American art. Among the famous paintings are Emanuel Leutze's *Washington Crossing the Delaware*, Albert Bierstadt's *The Rocky Mountains*, and a gallery devoted to Winslow Homer.

European paintings, sculpture, and decorative arts before 1800 include Botticelli's *Last Communion of St. Jerome*, Giovanni di Paolo's *Adoration of the Magi*, Rembrandt's *Self-Portrait, Aged 54*, and works by Bellini, Ingres, El Greco,

Holbein, Goya, and virtually any other famous painter you can name. Similarly, the collection of 19th-century European paintings and sculptures, including many works by such luminaries as Van Gogh, Monet, Renoir, and Degas, is stellar.

The Robert Lehman Collection, at the west end of the main floor, comprises fine early Italian and French Impressionist paintings, including several period rooms recreated from Lehman's home. The Michael C. Rockefeller Wing houses a very good collection of primitive art.

The Lila Acheson Wallace Wing, which is devoted to 20th-century art, is nearly as big as Midtown's Museum of Modern Art and remains one of the most popular sections of the Met. Featured here are paintings, sculptures, and decorative arts from Europe and America, including

> **Visitors should look out for special exhibitions at the Met; no extra ticket or admission fee is required.**

Picasso's *Gertrude Stein* and works by every major modern artist, including Jackson Pollock, Willem de Kooning, Edward Hopper, Georgia O'Keefe, Diego Rivera, Frank Stella, and Chuck Close.

Modern sculpture is on view in the roof garden overlooking Central Park, where there is a cafe in the summer. On top of all this, the Met has one of the best art bookstores in the US.

Neue Galerie

North of the Met (1048 Fifth Avenue at 86th Street) is the **Neue Galerie** (Sat–Mon 11am–6pm, Fri 11am–9pm), a fine new museum which specializes in German and Austrian art, featuring works by Klimt and various Bauhaus exponents. It is housed in an elegant mansion built in 1914 for the industrialist William Starr Miller by Carrère and Hastings, architects of the New York Public Library; the building was once occupied by society doyenne, Mrs Cornelius Vanderbilt III.

➤ Guggenheim Museum

At 89th Street is the **Solomon R. Guggenheim Museum** (Sun–Wed 9am–6pm, Fri–Sat 9am–8pm, closed Thurs, admission fee). The building, which was designed by Frank Lloyd Wright and opened in 1959, six months after his death, is now a New York landmark. An adjacent tower, based on Wright's original design, was opened in 1992, more than doubling the amount of exhibition space. The museum's most famous feature is perhaps not its paintings but the spiral ramp that connects the museum's six stories.

The permanent collection, built on Guggenheim's original private collection of contemporary paintings, includes works by such artists as Brancusi, Klee, Picasso, Miró, Calder, and Kandinsky (of whose work the museum has one of the world's largest collections). The Justin K. Thannhauser collection, in the annex, contains paintings by Renoir, Monet, Cézanne, Van Gogh, Gauguin, and Degas. The museum's collection is actually now spread somewhat thinly among its various branches in such disparate places as Bilbao, Venice, and Berlin.

Inside the Guggenheim

Across 89th Street is the **National Academy of Design**, whose permanent collection focuses on American art of the 19th and early 20th centuries.

And more museums...

Nearby, at 91st Street, is the **Cooper-Hewitt National Design Museum** (Tues 10am–9pm, Wed–Sat 10am– 5pm, Sun noon–5pm; admission fee). A branch of the Smithsonian Institute, the Cooper-Hewitt is more of a research institution than a museum. Though its collections are available to anyone by appointment, most of the vast holdings of furniture, wall-coverings, textiles, prints, drawings, and miscellaneous objects are not on display. But if there is a special exhibit that interests you, a visit to the mansion and its lovely gardens can be a treat.

At 92nd Street, the **Jewish Museum** (Sun, Mon, Wed, Thurs 11am–5.45pm, Tues 11am–8pm, closed Fri, Sat and Jewish holidays; admission fee), housed in a gothic mansion, is an important cultural and historical museum. Recently renovated, the museum holds an extensive collection of Judaica and exhibits the work of Jewish artists.

The **Museum of the City of New York** is located at 103rd Street. The collections of toy and Broadway memorabilia are a strength, as are the materials documenting New York City's history. The last institution on Museum Mile is **El Museo del Barrio** (Wed–Sun 11am–5pm), at 104th Street. Americans of Hispanic origin are scattered in many parts of New York City's five boroughs, but El Barrio – the Quarter – in East (or Spanish) Harlem was the first predominantly Puerto Rican district. The museum is devoted to Latin American culture and art.

CENTRAL PARK

The heart (some say the lungs) of Manhattan is **Central Park**, located between 59th and 125th streets and Fifth and Eighth avenues. This vast green space is half a mile wide and 2½ miles long (0.8 km x 4 km) and is one of the main places where New Yorkers go to play. On summer weekends, resi-

Relaxing in Central Park, the lungs of Manhattan

dents (and visitors) come by the thousands to play ball, skate, stroll, picnic, or listen to a concert. But the park is busy all week long and all year long. The park's designers were Frederick Law Olmstead and Calvert Vaux, and the project, which began in 1858, took almost 20 years to complete. Creating a usable public space from a huge, sparse, and rocky landscape was a remarkable achievement for the time and revolutionized landscape architecture. Amazingly, almost everything in the park, from the Great Lawn to the lakes, to the meadows and forest in the northern end, was constructed. The park is now partially supported, administered, and overseen by the Central Park Conservancy.

Park Highlights
Some highlights in the southern end of the park include **Wollman Rink** (mid-Park at 63rd Street), which is used for ice-skating in the winter and for roller- skating the rest of the

> Despite constant concerns about safety and occasional crimes, Central Park is actually one of the safest parts of Manhattan, though after dark there are more dangers than during daylight hours.

year. You can rent skates here. There's another skating rink in the northern end of the park, Lasker Rink (near 110th and Lenox Avenue).

Closer to Fifth Avenue is the small **Central Park Zoo** and **Tisch Children's Zoo** (in between is the George Delacorte Clock, which chimes the hours with musical animals). The highlights of the zoo include the sea-lion pool and polar bear house. The children's zoo has both a petting zoo and the 'Enchanted Forest.' The admission charge is for both zoos, which are open daily.

Another favorite in the southeast corner of the park is the historic **Carousel**, located mid-Park at 64th Street. It dates from 1908 and used to stand in a Coney Island amusement park. The carousel is a favorite of kids (OK…of adults as well). You can ride it from April through November, weather permitting.

You might also want to drop in at the **Dairy** (Tues–Sun 10am–5pm, to 4pm in winter), the Central Park visitors center (originally a real dairy) to find out what's going on in the park and to view the small historical exhibit. To the west is the Chess House, where you can watch the players absorbed in their game and perhaps take part yourself.

On the park's west side, near 66th Street, is **Tavern on the Green**, one of two restaurants in Central Park. The setting is dazzling, and the lighted gardens make a wonderful spot for a celebration, which won't come cheap. But set dinner menus will allow you to eat for around $50 with no time cut off, and there is a kid's menu. Nearby is the Sheep Meadow, one of New York's favorite places for Frisbee tossing and sunbathing in the summer; it's also a great place for a picnic. The sheep that used to graze here were originally housed in the Tavern on the Green building.

Right in the middle of the park, beginning at 66th Street, is the **Literary Walk**, lined with statues of writers you will, for the most part, recognize. The path leads up to the Mall, where there is a band shell, and ends at the **Bethesda Terrace and Fountain**, one of the park's best-known spots. On the lake here is the Loeb Boathouse, where there is a cafe in addition to a good (though also fairly expensive) restaurant open year-round. You can rent a boat or a bike near here in the summer. To the east is the **Conservatory Water**, a model-boat pond; at its northern end (at 74th Street) sits Central Park's most beloved sculpture, a bronze grouping of characters from Lewis Carroll's *Alice's Adventures in Wonderland*. To the west is **Strawberry Fields**, a memorial to John Lennon, who was killed nearby outside the Dakota apartment building at 72nd and Central Park West. North of this (at 80th Street) is the **Delacorte Theatre**, where you can see free plays during the summer. And in the center of the park is **Belvedere Castle**, which affords some great views; inside is a nature center and the park's weather station.

With Alice and the Mad Hatter

From the Castle, you'll be able to see the central part of the park, which features the **Great Lawn**, a huge expanse popular with sun-worshipers. On the east side is the Metropolitan Museum of Art *(see page 50)*, and just to the south **Cleopatra's Needle** (at 81st Street) a 3,600-year-old obelisk (not connected to Cleopatra), a gift from Egypt in the 19th century.

North of here are several other areas of note. The jogging path around the **Jacqueline Kennedy Onassis Reservoir** (mid-Park, north of 86th Street) is a favorite with runners. The **North Meadow** (mid-Park, at 96th Street) is another wide-open expanse, often the site of free concerts. At 104th Street is the **Conservatory Garden**, a group of formal gardens that are a popular location for weddings. And at the northern end of the park on the east side is the **Harlem Meer**, another lake.

Walkers in the park

There is always something going on in the park, from a concert to a rally to a bicycle race. You can take a walking tour of the park starting near 60th Street and Fifth Avenue (tel: 212-360 2727 for information and fees). The more active will be interested in ball fields, tennis courts, and other sporting opportunities. Since most of the park's roads are closed during weekends, strolling, biking, and skating are popular pastimes.

UPPER WEST SIDE

Beginning at Columbus Circle, where Broadway and Eighth Avenue (thereafter renamed Central Park West) converge, the Upper West Side stretches north to around Columbia University (about 110th Street); its western boundary is the Hudson River and Riverside Park, and its eastern boundary is Central Park. Colum-

The Lincoln Center for the Performing Arts

bus Circle is being reinvigorated by the construction of a massive business, retail, and entertainment complex that will include the offices of AOL-TimeWarner, CNN, and a major theater to be built on the site of the New York Coliseum.

Lincoln Center

The cultural epicenter of the Upper West Side is the **Lincoln Center for the Performing Arts**, which is bounded by 62nd and 66th streets (on the south and north), Amsterdam (the continuation of 10th Avenue) on the west, and Columbus (the continuation of 9th Avenue) on the east. The Center covers an area of 12 acres (5 hectares). The central plaza, a vast esplanade surrounding a fountain, acts as the focal point for the Center's three main buildings.

In the center is the **Metropolitan Opera House** (the other 'Met'), home to the Metropolitan Opera and the American Ballet Theater; it was designed by Wallace K. Harrison and completed in 1966 and can hold nearly 4,000 people. Two Chagall murals adorning the central lobby can be seen from the outside. To the left of the Met is the **New York State**

The Dakota

Theater, home of the New York City Ballet and the New York City Opera. Designed by architect Philip Johnson and built in 1964, it has a simple, stately facade complemented by a red-and-gold auditorium studded with crystal; the notoriously bad acoustics were recently upgraded through the installation of a modern sound system. To the right of the Met, opposite the New York State Theater, is **Avery Fisher Hall**, completed in 1962, which is primarily used for music concerts.

Just behind Avery Fisher Hall, to the right of the Met, you can make out the outline of **Lincoln Center Theater**; the structure was designed by Skidmore, Owings & Merrill, but the two theaters inside were designed by Finnish-born architect Eero Saarinen.

Farther back, but connected to Lincoln Center by a footbridge over West 65th Street, is the Juilliard School, one of the world's outstanding music conservatories.

Farther north are several interesting things to take a look at. The Beaux-Arts Ansonia building, at 2109 Broadway (73rd and 74th streets), is a notable apartment building. A little farther west, at the corner of 72nd and Central Park West, is the **Dakota**, which dates to 1884; it has been home to such rich and famous residents as Lauren Bacall, John Lennon and Yoko Ono, and Roberta Flack.

A few blocks farther north, between 76th and 77th streets, is the **New-York Historical Society** (Tues–Sat 11am–5pm; admission fee), the oldest museum in New York (the second-oldest in the US). In addition to documents and artifacts of historical interest, the Society's collection includes American fine and decorative arts.

Natural History Museum

The huge building on Central Park West at 79th Street is the **American Museum of Natural History** (Sun–Thurs 10am–5.45pm, Fri–Sat 10am–8.45pm; admission fee), another of New York's oldest museums, dating to 1869. Once a pretty stuffy place full of old dinosaur bones and dusty taxidermy displays, much of the museum has been renovated and reinvented over the past few years; crowds are drawn to the new **Hayden Planetarium**, the centerpiece of the Frederick Phineas and Sandra Priest Rose Center for Earth and Space. The Hall of Planet Earth is also a part of this newest section.

Among the dinosaurs at the Natural History Museum

The new Hayden Planetarium

With tens of millions of specimens and artifacts, the museum is a repository for knowledge of virtually any aspect of earth's natural history and development. The creaking dioramas are still there and now seem quaint. But the more recently refurbished parts of the museum, including the Fossil Halls (covering everything from dinosaurs to mammals) and the Hall of Biodiversity (which now includes a rare giant squid caught in late 1997), have the most up-to-the-minute scientific information and wonderful state-of-the-art exhibitions.

Don't miss the full-size model of a blue whale, the Star of India (the largest sapphire ever discovered), and the Barosaurus in the Theodore Roosevelt Rotunda on Central Park West (it's the tallest free-standing dinosaur exhibit in the world). Tours of the collection's highlights are given regularly throughout the day. The museum also has an Imax theater.

Columbia University Area
Many visitors are surprised to find one of the largest Gothic cathedrals in the world in New York City. The **Episcopal Cathedral Church of St John the Divine**, at Amsterdam Avenue and 112th Street (open daily 8am–6pm), was begun in 1892 and is still unfinished. You can see the scaffolding

around the unfinished spire. The church is known for its jazz and choral music series, as well as its rotating art exhibits.

Beyond the cathedral, at 116th and Broadway, lies the campus of **Columbia University**. Founded in 1754 as King's College, Columbia is New York City's representative in the Ivy League. A private university, its schools of law and

> If you're traveling with children, you may want to consider visiting the Children's Museum of Manhattan, at 212 W. 83rd Street (Amsterdam and Broadway). There are daily programs as well as interactive exhibits and an activity center, including a play area for toddlers. The museum is open Tues–Sun 10am–5pm.

journalism and the teacher's college are widely recognized for their excellence. (The School of Journalism administers the Pulitzer Prizes each year.) The campus is striking. Right across Broadway stands Barnard College, Columbia University's affiliated women's college.

Not far away, in Riverside Park at West 122nd Street, is **Grant's Tomb**, the mausoleum of General Ulysses S. Grant, Commander-in-Chief of the Union Army in the Civil War and US President from 1869 to 1877, and his wife, Julia Dent Grant. After the war, the general settled in New York City and worked on Wall Street and died here in July 1885. Administered by the National Park Service, the mausoleum, which is the biggest in the US, contains a museum devoted to Grant's life, which is open daily except for Federal holidays and is free.

HARLEM

Harlem is undergoing many, mostly positive changes right now. Though it is still the one of the most economically depressed sections of Manhattan, several large commercial building projects and many more residential ones are under way. Often considered the spiritual capital of Black America, Harlem is a vital and varied community, with its rich, poor, and middle-income sections, historical and cultural landmarks, attractive homes, and, still, its share of sadly run-down streets. A popular way to see Harlem is on one of the hop-on-hop-off double-decker bus tours or a specialized tour that often includes lunch and a gospel music performance; tours that include a Sunday church service are especially popular. For more information, *see page 84.*

Harlem begins north of Central Park at 110th Street and extends to 178th Street, bounded on the west by Morningside Heights and Washington Heights and on the north and east by the Harlem River, which connects the Hudson and East rivers. The neighborhood's commercial center is 125th Street, where you'll find the historic **Apollo Theater** (253 West 125th Street). The Harlem USA retail complex has recently opened at the corner of Federick Douglass Boulevard and 125th Street.

Historic District

Founded by Dutch settlers, Harlem remained a village for a long time. As immigrants moved into the Lower East Side, many middle-class families moved north to Harlem. The influx of black families started around 1900 and reached its

---

Harlem's Churches

Central Harlem is known for its beautiful churches. The Abyssinian Baptist Church at 132 West 138th Street was founded in 1808; its current Harlem home dates to 1923. Also in the area are the Mother AME Zion Church, at 140 West 137th Street, which is the oldest black congregation in New York. St. Phillip's Episcopal Church is a striking neo-Gothic building at 214 West 134th Street.

height around 1920, when the area became a cultural hub and home to prominent artists and writers associated with the Harlem Renaissance. Historic row houses of this period are preserved in the **St Nicholas Historic District** between Adam Clayton Powell, Jr. Boulevard and Frederick Douglass Boulevard on 138th and 139th streets.

There are several prominent cultural institutions in the area. The **Studio Museum in Harlem**, 144 West 125th Street, at Lenox Avenue (Wed–Fri 10am–5pm and Sat–Sun 1–6pm; admission fee) is dedicated to African-American,

One of Harlem's many places of worship

Caribbean, and contemporary and traditional African art. At Lenox Avenue and 135th Street, the **Schomburg Center for Research in Black Culture** (tel: 212-491 2200), a branch of the New York Public Library and an art museum, possesses one of the world's most important collections covering black history and African-American culture. Open daily.

At 287 Convent Avenue (141st and 142nd streets) is the **Hamilton Grange National Memorial**, which was the early 19th-century home of Alexander Hamilton; unfortunately, you can only pass by to take a look, but the entire area, which was originally his farm and is now known as **Hamilton Heights**, is a historic district. This area includes the row

If you yearn for something to eat in Harlem, there are many good choices. The place that says Harlem for most people is Sylvia's (328 Lenox Avenue, at 127th Street, tel: 212-966 0660), where you can sample typical South Carolina fare; its Sunday gospel brunch is especially popular. Another is Charles' Southern Style Kitchen (2841 Frederick Douglass Boulevard, between 151st and 152nd streets, tel: 212-926 4313).

houses on Sugar Hill, which is roughly the area between St. Nicholas and Edgecombe avenues and 143rd to 155th streets. The stately **Morris-Jumel Mansion** and gardens (1765) at 65 Jumel Terrace (at 161st Street; tel: 212-923 8008) exhibits period furniture in a beautifully restored setting (open Wed–Sun 10am–4pm).

The 1908 Beaux-Arts **Audubon Terrace** complex, on Broadway between 155th and 156th streets, is home to several cultural institutions. There's the **American Academy of Arts and Letters** (tel: 212-368 5900), which has seasonal exhibitions but is otherwise not open to the public. And also two museums: the **American Numismatic Society** has a large collection of coins (tel: 212-234 3130), and the **Hispanic Society of America** (tel: 212-926 2234) has a permanent collection that includes rare books and manuscripts and works by Goya and El Greco. Both are closed on Monday and ask for a donation for admission.

Washington Heights

Above Harlem, Manhattan narrows to a little sliver made up of **Washington Heights** and Inwood. Both are primarily residential neighborhoods, but there are a couple of interesting attractions. Washington Heights is predominately a Dominican neighborhood; long known as a drug-seller's haven, it is beginning to clean up its act.

The Cloisters

Beyond Washington Heights is **Fort Tryon Park**, a 66-acre (26-hectare) park of landscaped and terraced hills, which begins at 190th Street. From the subway stop (A line) here, it's possible to walk through the park or take a city bus to **The Cloisters** (Tues–Sun 9.30am–4.45pm, until 5.15pm in summer; admission fee). Part of the Metropolitan Museum (your admission to the Met also gives you same-day admission here), this branch is devoted to Medieval art and architecture. It is built around parts of several actual cloisters and other medieval structures. The views of the Hudson River from the outdoor terraces are breathtaking, and the gardens provide a great place to sit in reflective solitude.

Medieval Cloisters

Housed within The Cloisters are several genuine masterpieces, including the wood sculpture *Enthroned Virgin and Child*, a set of 'nine heroes' tapestries, a 12th-century carved ivory cross, and the museum's most popular holding, a set of tapestries depicting the *Hunt for the Unicorn*.

Not far away is the **Dyckman Farmhouse Museum** at 4881 Broadway (Tues–Sun 11am–4pm; donation requested). This is the only remaining Dutch colonial farmhouse in Manhattan. If you're in the neighborhood, it's worth a detour.

OTHER NEIGHBORHOODS

The Lower East Side

At the turn of the 20th century, the Lower East Side of Manhattan was the most densely populated place in the US, home to around half a million Russian and Eastern European Jewish immigrants, many of whom had fled the porgroms that followed the assassination of Tsar Alexander II in 1881. The remnants of the old Jewish neighborhood are located on the northeast side of Chinatown, beyond Hester Street, the site of the Jewish market at the end of the 19th century. Simply follow Hester Street east and then walk north along **Orchard Street**, and you'll see a shadow of the market's heyday mixed in with hip eateries and new clubs. Dormant on the Jewish Sabbath from Friday evening to Saturday at sunset, the place springs back to life on Sunday.

The Lower East Side Tenement Museum

In this New World ghetto, the cornerstone of the economy was the 'needle trade.' Payment was on a piecework basis, and working conditions and pay were appalling. Those who didn't enter the trade often worked as peddlers or pushcart vendors, selling produce or cheap clothing in the markets on Hester Street and Orchard Street. The best introduction to the area is at the **Lower East Side Tenement Museum** at 97 Orchard Street (at Broome Street; Tues–Fri noon–5pm, Sat–Sun 11am–5pm). Located in a 19th-century tenement, the museum also conducts walking tours with commentary. It has a free historical gallery, along with three restored cramped apartments that can be toured with a guide.

Chinatown brims with exotic produce

Chinatown

Of all the ethnic neighborhoods that were established on New York's Lower East Side, it's the Chinese enclave that has continued to thrive. The narrow shops sell ivory and jade jewelry as well as bootleg designer watches and the usual souvenirs; grocers display exotic Chinese produce; and innumerable restaurants feature regional specialties.

Well over 200,000 people live in bustling Chinatown, a loosely defined area embracing Canal Street, Chatham Square, and Mott Street. The earliest Chinese arrivals came to America in the 19th century, during the California Gold Rush and the period of railway construction; most immigrants today come directly from the Fujian province in southern China. Near Chatham Square, at the corner of Division Street and Bowery, stands a 1983 bronze statue of Confucius, and south of the square, a few steps down St James Place, are some of New York's oldest monuments, barely a dozen tombstones, the touching remnants of the **Shearith Israel Cemetery**, founded here in 1656 by New York's first immigrants, Spanish and Portuguese Jews.

Little Italy

'Little' is certainly the operative word here, as this area has now been largely subsumed by Chinatown. The stretch of Mulberry Street from Canal to Grand is still home to several Italian restaurants and expensive coffee bars. In the summer, especially on weekends, it's a pleasant place to stroll, buy a souvenir, and have a plate of pasta and a glass of house wine al fresco. There are still some good bakeries and grocers here, though some of them, too, are now Chinese. The district is at its liveliest during the ten-day Feast of San Gennaro in early September *(see page 96)*. But if you find yourself in the neighborhood, you might want to take a stroll over to the old **Police Headquarters** at the corner of Center and Grand streets; this is the building in which Theodore Roosevelt served as New York City's police commissioner. The inhabitants are now the tenants of the luxury condominiums created in the late 1980s; TR's former office is probably someone's boudoir now.

SoHo and TriBeCa

SoHo (South of Houston) is the area bound by Houston Street, Broadway, Canal Street, and the Hudson River. It has become the Village's chic southern neighbor, with expensive cafes, restaurants, art galleries, and shops selling the very latest in fashion and housewares. Its history has followed the pattern of Greenwich Village. Artists who couldn't afford the rents after the Village's commercialization moved south to the derelict lofts and warehouse floors of the then industrial district. The most successful were able to install kitchens, bathrooms, and comfortable interiors, while others made do with bare walls and floors for the sake of ample space and light. Now the same lofts sell in the multi-million-dollar range, and it's a fight between real artists and real millionaires.

Warehouse space in SoHo

The main thing to do down here is to browse in the galleries, stop and relax at the many outdoor cafés and restaurants, and shop. Broadway is the most mainstream shopping street. But there are also some highly worthwhile attractions. They include the **New Museum of Contemporary Art** (Wed–Fri and Sun noon–6pm, Sat noon–8pm; admission fee; free on Thurs evening 6pm–8pm), the city's premier museum of contemporary art showcasing an enormous range of innovative art from around the world – from paintings and sculptures to installations and videos.

A fun place for kids is the **Scholastic Bookstore**, 557 Broadway (Mon–Sat 10am–8pm, Sun noon–6pm). In addition to books, toys, CD Roms, videos and games, it has creative displays featuring *Clifford The Big Red Dog*, *Harry Potter*, *Miss Spider*, *Captain Underpants*, *The Magic School Bus*, and other Scholastic favorites. Events, activities, and storytellings are held nearly every day.

West Broadway is the liveliest of the SoHo streets. Here you'll find the choicest shops and galleries, though there are significant selections of both on the side streets and now all over the area.

After SoHo became too expensive, the dealers moved in, and the artists moved out, many heading southwest to the derelict warehouses of the TriBeCa (Triangle Below Canal) neighborhood, which in its turn has seen the opening of many art galleries, fashionable restaurants, and trendy boutiques. As the rents began to sky-rocket, many of the artists migrated across the river to Williamsburg in Brooklyn; even some of the art dealers have moved out.

TriBeCa's high-priced loft-style real estate is home to many high profile New Yorkers. But perhaps the district's most ardent resident-supporter is actor Robert DeNiro. He opened his restaurant TriBeCa Grill, which is still going strong, and has also instituted the TriBeCa Film Festival.

➤ Greenwich Village

'The Village,' as **Greenwich Village** is usually called, has been separate, casual, and very different from the rest of the city ever since its beginnings. In colonial times it really was a distinct village called Greenwich, which became a neighborhood of conservative Georgian brick houses and carriage barns in back-alley mews. A few of these houses remain, mostly on **Bedford Street** and the streets around it, but conservative the Village isn't. It got its bohemian reputation after World War I, when artists and writers who found cheap lodgings, inexpensive restaurants, and speakeasies scattered throughout the Village, decided to call it home. Later, the Village became the center for New York's gay community, which to some degree has moved north to Chelsea.

The Village is roughly the area from 14th Street down to Houston and west of Broadway. The area's heart is **Washington Square Park**, which has become the de facto campus quadrangle for **New York University**, which controls much of the real estate east of 6th Avenue and south of 14th Street to Houston. The park's famous arch was designed by architect Stanford White and erected in 1889 to mark the centenary of George Washington's inauguration as president.

Hidden away behind these buildings surrounding Washington Square are two private lanes that used to lead to the stables belonging to the area's wealthy residents: **Washington Mews**, one block up Fifth Avenue from the park on your right, and **MacDougal Alley**, just a few steps up MacDougal Street from the northwest corner of the square.

Bleecker Street with its craft and curio shops, antique stores, cafes, and tiny restaurants has long been the main

Washington Mews

Washington Square Park

shopping strip of the neighborhood. The highest concentration of gay and lesbian businesses and bars is still on **Christopher Street**, west of 7th Avenue South. The **Stonewall**, at 53 Christopher Street, stands roughly on the spot of the original Stonewall Inn, which was the site of the riots in 1968 that led to the modern gay rights movement. You may wish to make at least two trips to the Village – by day to shop and see the sights, and at night to catch the atmosphere, have dinner, and hit one of the jazz clubs or bars.

East Village

A separate community, the **East Village** extends east from Broadway to Avenue D and the East River. Much less affluent than Greenwich Village to the west, this neighborhood is nevertheless seeing signs of gentrification, though it's still the place you are likely to see a multiply-pierced, blue-haired youth just hanging out. You'll find small boutiques, restaurants, and interesting shops that can't afford the other downtown rents. If there is any real bohemian spirit left in Manhattan, it may be here. A walk down St. Mark's Place or Avenue A, the liveliest streets, can almost take you back to the 1960s; stop for a rest and some great people-watching in Tomkins Square.

On Lafayette Street, just to the south of Cooper Square, stands the building that once housed the first public library of New York. Nowadays it's the seat of the **Joseph Papp Public Theater**, which actually contains several theaters and is the home of the New York Shakespeare Festival. Joe's Pub, off the main lobby, is a new and popular cabaret. Nearby is the Great Hall of the Cooper Union, the center of the free university established by Peter Cooper in 1859.

Those interested in historic buildings might stop by **St Mark's-in-the-Bowery**, built in 1799 on the very spot where the Stuyvesant family chapel once stood (at 10th Street at 2nd Avenue). It is now a charming church with some noteworthy stained-glass windows – and an extremely lively congregation, often hosting music or dance performances.

Chelsea
The area between 14th and 23rd streets west of Sixth Avenue is once again a thriving neighborhood after many years of

Village Voices

Since the Art Nouveau period, Greenwich Village has been one big 'village of genius' and home of the artistic avant-garde. The radical paper *Masses*, whose contributors included Maxim Gorki, Bertrand Russell, and John Reed, had its offices here. In 1914, Gertrude Vanderbilt Whitney opened a gallery and provided a platform for contemporary artists, much of whose work was highly controversial. In 1916, members of the Playwrights' Theater settled on MacDougal Street and soon achieved fame – Eugene O'Neill among them.

After World War II the Bohemian image of 'the Village' persisted. In the 1950s, the beatnik movement flowered (Jack Kerouac and Allen Ginsberg); in the 1960s and early '70s the area was home to hippies and anti-Vietnam war activists (Abbie Hoffman and Jerry Rubin).

Sunset stroll at Chelsea Piers

decline. It's also one of the trendiest gay neighborhoods in Manhattan. Stroll up Eighth Avenue, where you'll find gay bars and boutiques, as well as restaurants catering to all types. The **Joyce Theater**, at 19th Street, is one of the main venues in town for modern dance. On 23rd Street, between Seventh and Eighth avenues, is the Chelsea Hotel; originally a cooperative building, it now houses artists permanently and other guests only nightly. In far west Chelsea, you'll find the **Chelsea Piers** sports and entertainment complex along the Hudson River from 17th to 23rd streets.

Seventh Avenue is quieter, but you'll still find many restaurants and stores. Loehmann's, on Seventh Avenue at 16th Street, is a prime source for deeply discounted designer clothing. Sixth Avenue from 18th to 23rd streets was once known as the 'Ladies Mile.' For many years, the massive storefronts stood derelict; now they are inhabited by such retailers as Old Navy and Bed, Bath, and Beyond.

EXCURSIONS TO THE OUTER BOROUGHS

Brooklyn

Brooklyn, which actually has a larger population than Manhattan, is one of the largest urban centers in America. It's worth a trip over the East River to see some of the sights. One easy-to-reach destination is **Brooklyn Heights**, the neighborhood closest to Manhattan. Take the subway numbers 2 or 3 to Clark Street, or simply walk across the Brooklyn Bridge from the east side of City Hall Park, from where the view is unparalleled.

Rising above the East River, the Heights is an attractive area of 19th-century brownstones and picturesque streets, long popular with writers and artists (although today the rents are as high as in Manhattan). The **Promenade** (three blocks down Clark Street from the bridge), is an esplanade with one of the most impressive views in town, including both the Manhattan skyline and the Statue of Liberty. Late afternoon is a good time to go, when the office towers of Lower Manhattan start to glow in the light of the setting sun. At the end of the Promenade, walk south along Hicks Street, a shady street in a quarter that has barely changed since 1860.

Brooklyn Heights facade

If you are interested in subways and how they are run, then a trip to the **New York Transit Museum** (tel: 718/243 3060) may be in order. Housed in an authentic 1930s subway station at the corner of Boerum Place and Schermerhorn Street, the museum, renovated in 2002–3, has a great variety of galleries and exhibits, many of which have interactive components. They also have an annex museum/store in Grand Central Terminal *(see page 42)*.

The **Brooklyn Museum of Art** (200 Eastern Parkway; open Wed–Fri 10am–5pm, Sat–Sun 11am–6pm; admission fee) is one of the largest museums in New York, with exceptional collections of Egyptian, Asian, Persian, and pre-Columbian art. The American furniture collections are also interesting, though certainly not as large as those at the Met. And there are some good examples of 19th-century painting, with a focus on New York painters. Take the 2 or 3 subway to Eastern Parkway.

Brooklyn Botanical Garden

Adjacent to the museum is the **Brooklyn Botanical Garden**. Not to be confused with the much larger New York Botanical Garden in the Bronx *(see page 80)*, it's nevertheless a peaceful place to stroll while admiring the flowers and trees. A combined visit to the museum and the garden is a nice way to spend an unhurried day outside of Manhattan.

The Bronx

For quite a while now, the Bronx has had a reputation for crime and urban decay. While there are certainly parts of the Bronx where this is still true, visitors who haven't been here lately will be surprised. Several attractions make it worth a special trip to New York's only borough on the US mainland.

One such attraction is the **Bronx Zoo** (open Mon–Fri 10am–5pm; weekends until 5.30pm; Nov–Mar 10am–4.30pm; admission fee, free Wed). At its most inviting from May through October, when all of the sections are

In the grounds of Bronx Zoo

open, the zoo is actually open every day of the year (reduced admission during winter), and there is always something interesting going on. There are 6,000 animals of almost 600 species. At the Congo Gorilla Forest (separate fee) you get to meet the zoo's gorillas up close and personal. Though they are behind glass, there is still a lot of interaction with the crowd, and when there are fewer people, it's quite an intimate experience. Other popular exhibits are Wild Asia and its Bengali Express monorail (where you can see tigers; separate fee); Jungle World, the World of Birds, Children's Zoo (separate fee), and the World of Darkness (nocturnal animals), and, in the summer, the Butterfly Zone (separate fee). This is undoubtedly one of the world's great zoos, and a day here can be quite memorable.

To get to the zoo, take the 2 subway to Pelham Parkway, and walk west to the Bronx Parkway entrance; this section of the track is elevated, and you'll be able to see the park on the left side of the train as you approach the station. Alternatively, you can take Metro North from Grand Central to Fordham station then the B-9 bus to the Southern Boulevard Entrance.

Adjacent to the zoo is the **New York Botanical Garden** (open Tues–Sun 10am–6pm, in the winter until 4pm only), a striking 250-acre (100-hectare) national landmark. Highlights include several specialty gardens, an orchid collection, a 40-acre (16-hectare) uncut, almost virgin forest, and the recently refurbished Enid A. Haupt Conservatory. The garden has a small entry fee, and for an additional fee, you can take a narrated tram tour. To get to the garden, take Metro North from Grand Central to the New York Botanical Garden stop; alternatively, you can take the D or 4 subway to Bedford Park Boulevard, but this requires a long walk or additional bus ride.

> **Baseball fans may be interested to know that tours of Yankee Stadium are conducted at various times throughout the year, though not always during baseball season. You must make an advance reservation through Ticketmaster (tel: 212-307 1212) or by calling the Yankee tour office (tel: 718-597 4531). The one-hour tour begins at the press gate and costs $8, $4 for seniors and children under 12. To get to the stadium, take the B, D, or 4 subway to 161st Street.**

Queens

The most diverse borough of the five that make up New York, Queens has several attractions that will interest visitors.

During the silent movie era, Queens was the equivalent of today's Hollywood – the center of the motion-picture industry – and movies and TV shows are still produced at the Kaufman-Astoria studios here. Located in the studio complex, on 35th Avenue at 36th Street in Astoria, the **American Museum of the Moving Image** (Tues–Fri noon–5pm, Sat–Sun 11am–6pm; admission fee) celebrates this early movie history and explores the art, technique, and technology of film, television, and digital

Long lines at MOMA QNS

media, examining their impact on society. To reach the museum, take the R subway to Steinway Street or the N to 36th Avenue and walk to the museum.

In Long Island City, just across from midtown Manhattan, is the **P.S. 1 Contemporary Art Center** (22–25 Jackson Avenue at 46th Street; Thur–Fri noon–6pm; admission fee), the largest contemporary art museum in New York and well worth a visit for its cutting-edge exhibitions.

But the biggest draw for art lovers in Queens is now MOMA QNS (33rd Street at Queens Boulevard; Sat–Mon, Thur 10am–5pm, Fri 10am–7.45pm, admission fee). The bulk of the famous Museum of Modern Art collection has been transferred here while renovation work, due for completion in 2005, is carried out on the main Manhattan premises *(see page 39)*; the former Swingline staple factory has been remodelled as an excellent gallery space. To get there, take the 7 local subway train direct to 33rd Street.

WHAT TO DO

GUIDED TOURS

Visitors, especially if they are in New York for the first time, should consider taking a tour to become familiar with the city. Happily, there are many different options. If you want a walking tour, several choices are available, and since the schedules for these change so often, the best place to see what's going on is to check in *Time Out New York*.

By Bus
Some of the more popular tours offered in New York are on double-decker buses. Several companies offer these hop-on-hop-off tours, which provide a convenient way to hit the major sights. The only disadvantages are the price and the traffic, yet for those visitors who don't want to deal with New York's transit system on their own, these are an ideal option. One choice is **Gray Line** (terminal at 8th Avenue and 42nd Street, tel: 212-397 2600; <www.graylinenewyork.com>). The tours can be combined with various other options, such as boat and helicopter tours as well as admissions to popular attractions.

By Boat
Since Manhattan is an island, you can also see the city by water. **Circle Line** (tel: 212-563 3200; <www.circleline.com>) offers various options, including 3-hour cruises around the island. Most of their cruises leave from Pier 83 at 42nd Street and Twelfth Avenue, though there are also some departures from South Street Seaport's Pier 16. **NY Waterway** (tel: 800-533 3779; <www.nywaterway.com>) runs regular tours from Pier 78 at 38th Street and Twelfth Avenue as well as a 'disco' cruise from South Street Seaport's Pier 17.

By Air

A more expensive option is to see Manhattan by helicopter. Two companies offer these tours: **Liberty Helicopter Tours** (tel: 212-967 6464; <www.libertyhelicopters.com>) leave from either Pier 6 (near the end of Whitehall Street in Lower Manhattan) or 30th Street and Twelfth Avenue (two-person minimum). **Helicopter Flight Services**, Inc. (tel: 212-355 0801; <www.heliny.com>) leave from Pier 6 downtown. You can also take a seaplane tour from SeaAir NY (tel: 212-681 4779; <www.seaairny.com>). The 30-minute tours leave from the Skyport at 23rd Street and the East River.

Themed Tours

Adventure on a Shoestring, 300 West 53rd Street, tel: (212) 265 2663. Tours through particular neighborhoods and also special themes, e.g. sites with literary associations.

Municipal Art Society, 457 Madison Avenue, tel: (212) 935 3960. Tours focussing on history and architecture.

Bite of the Apple Central Park Bicycle Tours, 2 Columbus Circle, tel: (212) 541 8759. Tours across Central Park.

Broadway Open House, tel: (212) 239 6200. A 2-hour tour of landmark Broadway. Theaters and introduction to the Great White Way.

Harlem Spirituals/New York Visions, 690 Eighth Avenue, tel: (212) 391 0900. Harlem jazz and gospel tours, plus sightseeing in Brooklyn and the Bronx.

Harlem Your Way, 128 West 130th Street, tel: (212) 690 1687. Walking tours of Harlem, including gospel churches and jazz clubs.

Urban Park Rangers, 1234 Fifth Avenue, tel: (212) 360 2774. Tours with nature themes in various parks. For Central Park tours, call the Ranger Station at (212) 628 2345.

Wall Street Walking Tour, tel: (212) 606 4064. History of the world's financial capital, Thur and Sat at noon.

Macy's, the largest department store in the world

SHOPPING

If you can't afford to buy (and in the trendy stores on Madison Avenue that may very well be the case), you can at least window-shop. Virtually anything is available in Manhattan for a price, which is sometimes, though certainly not always, a bargain.

When and Where to Shop

Most stores are open Monday to Saturday from 10am to 6pm or longer. Many shops and department stores are open late at least one night a week, usually on Thursday. All the large department stores are open on Sunday afternoons.

If you are looking for inexpensive New York souvenirs, avoid Midtown and the areas around major tourist attractions (like the Empire State Building). Instead, try 14th Street, particularly between Fifth and Sixth Avenues, as well as Chinatown, especially the north side of Canal and the blocks on either side of Mulberry. Greenwich Village can still be an interesting place to shop; browse the quirky smaller stores along Bleecker Street (antique shops are concentrated on the western stretch, beyond Christopher). SoHo, a major weekend destination for area shoppers, is the home of fine art galleries and designer-clothing and home-furnishings stores. There are also quite a few boutique clothing stores in Chelsea. And, of course, don't forget the East Village.

The reliable standard shopping neighborhoods have always been Fifth Avenue above 50th Street (for decades very chic but now increasingly more predictable and loaded with chain and theme stores) and Madison Avenue from Midtown to the Upper East Side (home to some very luxurious, high-end shops).

What to Buy

Art and antiques: Art galleries and antiques shops are found throughout the city. The largest concentrations are along East 57th Street and up Madison Avenue to 84th Street. A movement away from SoHo, where there are still some galleries, has led to a boom in new galleries in west

---

Museum Shops

American Folk Art Museum, Lincoln Square. Rural crafts and toys from around the country.

Metropolitan Museum of Art Gift Shop, in the museum on Fifth Avenue and also at Rockefeller Center (15 West 49th Street). Art books, posters, jewelry, reproductions.

The MoMA Design Store, 11 West 53rd Street. Designer furniture and household articles.

The Museum of the City of New York, 5th Avenue at 103rd Street. The place to go to find old prints of the city.

Chelsea. There are some good antique stores on Bleecker Street, west of Christopher Street in Greenwich Village. One institution worth visiting for its wide range of choices is the Manhattan Art and Antiques Center (1050 2nd Avenue at 56th Street), which boasts some 85 stalls selling ceramics, crystal, and assorted bric-a-brac.

Chelsea's the place to go for good flea markets, both open-air and enclosed. Try the Chelsea Antiques Building at 110 West 25th Street (6th and 7th avenues), where you'll find over 100 dealers. There's also an open-air flea market on Grand Street at Centre Street.

Clothing: You really can find bargains among the prodigious array of clothes in the department stores, especially during end-of-season sales. But it would be a shame to limit your search to the bigger stores. Head to Madison Avenue above 60th Street for high-fashion boutiques, to SoHo (expensive) and the East Village (less expensive) for more daring designs, to Fifth Avenue for reliable luxury labels, and to Chelsea (particularly along Eighth Avenue) for club-wear. The best place for discount designer clothing is Century 21 (22 Cortlandt Street, between Broadway and Church); almost everything starts at half price, and sometimes there are some real bargains.

Computers and Electronics: Approach the so-called 'discount' electronics stores to be found all over Midtown with a critical eye; sales techniques can be high-pressure, dealers have been known to be unscrupulous, and the prices are not always as good as you might think. Many of these dealers are reputable, however, and real bargains can be found if you know what you're looking for. New Yorkers shop at J&R Music World (23 Park Row, near City Hall), where you can find absolutely everything and the sales staff is knowledgeable; adjacent J&R stores sell cameras, computers, and anything else electronic you can imagine. Computer stores are

> Macy's, established in New York City in 1858, is the world's largest store at 2.1 million square feet (189,000 square meters). It stocks over 500,000 items.

concentrated on Fifth Avenue, above 20th Street.

Department Stores: Macy's (34th and Broadway) and Bloomingdale's (59th and Lexington) have everything; Lord and Taylor (38th and Fifth Avenue) is a little smaller. Barney's (61st and Madison) is known for cutting-edge fashion and upscale home furnishings. Saks Fifth Avenue (at 50th) is strictly high fashion for ladies who lunch and their gentlemen, as is Bergdorf Goodman (57th and 5th Avenue). Takashimaya is a very chic Japanese alternative (5th Avenue near 54th).

Jewelry: Hit the Diamond District on West 47th for all prices and styles but not always bargains; Fifth Avenue above 50th Street is the location for the high-end jewelers (Cartier, Tiffany, Harry Winston, Bulgari, Van Cleef and Arpels). Small boutiques in SoHo, Greenwich Village, and the East Village are your best bets for hand-made originals (some of which can be quite nice).

Records and Books: It's worth getting an eyeful of the enormous Virgin Megastore in Times Square (at 45th Street), though the one at Union Square (14th and Broadway) is a more pleasant place to shop. Choose from vast selections at the Tower Records on Broadway at 66th Street near Lincoln Center (especially good for Broadway and classical) and at Broadway and West 4th Street in Greenwich Village (for imports and less mainstream music), and at the large HMV store on 42nd Street between 7th and 8th Avenues, and elsewhere (mostly mainstream). Go to both St Mark's Place and Bleecker (around Carmine) for concentrations of used CD stores.

In the book realm, Barnes and Noble has superstores catering to the masses (Union Square North, 6th Avenue at

22nd Street, Broadway at 66th Street, Lexington at 86th Street), as does Borders (Park Avenue and 57th Street, 2nd Avenue and 32nd Street). The Gotham Book Mart at 41 West 47th Street is the most celebrated independent bookstore in the city, redolent with literary tradition and a great place to browse. Specialty bookstores all over the city cater to such tastes as theater (Drama Book Shop at 240 West 40th), mysteries (Partners and Crime on Greenwich Avenue), science fiction (Forbidden Planet on Broadway at 13th Street), and art (Rizzoli on West Broadway or any museum store). Young readers are enchanted by Books of Wonder (18th Street west of 5th Avenue). For used books and out-of-print titles don't forget the renowned Strand Book Store (Broadway at 12th Street), the country's largest second-hand book dealer.

FAO **Schwartz for the ultimate in toys**

Toys: The ultimate toy store is FAO Schwarz (5th Avenue at 58th), where, should you feel like it, a doll's house will be yours to keep for a mere $10,000. Penny Whistle (1283 Madison Avenue at 91st) is an interesting boutique.

Only in New York: The unassuming Kiehl's (3rd Avenue between 13th and 14th) puts the Body Shop to shame for health and beauty products. Zabar's (Broadway between 80th and 81st) and Dean & DeLuca (560 Broadway in SoHo) are fancy-food heavens. Broadway Panhandler (Broome between Greene and Wooster) has everything for your kitchen. Folks come from all over the world to shop at Kate's Paperie (Broadway between Prince and Spring). Honestly, if M&J Buttons (6th Avenue between 37th and 38th) doesn't have the one you're looking for, it probably doesn't exist.

NIGHTLIFE

The night is yet young

They don't call it the city that never sleeps for nothing. Whether you are interested in theater, the performing arts, a hot dance club, or just a quiet drink, you'll have plenty of opportunities to have fun once the sun goes down. There's no way to cover the entire New York nightlife scene in these few short paragraphs. But luckily, there are plenty of resources for finding out what's going on either before you arrive or once you've gotten to New York. The best places to find out what's going on during your stay are the Friday or Sunday *New York Times* (for mainstream events), *The New Yorker* or *New York* magazines (good for arts and more sophisticated clubs and bars), the *Village Voice* (an alternative weekly paper, especially strong on music), or *Time Out New York* (a weekly magazine with wide coverage of everything).

Tickets to most events can be purchased from Ticketmaster (tel: 800-755 4000 or <www.ticketmaster.com>), which charges a hefty service charge on top of the already hefty cost of the ticket itself.

Theater

One of the most popular activities for visitors is to take in a Broadway or off-Broadway show. Broadway theaters are concentrated in the Times Square area, but smaller off-Broadway houses, where the offerings are increasingly interesting, are located all over town. Tickets for current hits must be booked ahead, sometimes months ahead. Curtain times are generally 8pm for evening performances, 2pm for matinees, which are usually on Wednesday, Saturday, and Sunday. Be prepared for sticker shock; the top shows charge $80 for their best seats, and American theaters often do not follow the lead of the world by charging less for the less desirable seats.

Classical Music and Dance

New York offers every kind of music imaginable, from opera and classical music to jazz, pop, blues, country, and reggae.

Discount Theater Tickets

Discount theater tickets (25–50 percent off) for same-day performances can be purchased at two TKTS locations in Manhattan. The most popular is in Duffy Square at 47th Street, which sells evening tickets after 3pm and matinee tickets after 11am daily. The other location is at South Street Seaport; it's open Mon–Sat 11am–5.30pm (here they sell matinee tickets the day before the performance, and lines are usually shorter than in Times Square). Note that only cash or traveler's checks are accepted, and they make no exceptions.

Nights on Broadway

Admission to many of the concerts is free: the summer concerts in Central Park, for instance, or the lunch-time concerts held in the Financial District and midtown, which liven up the day for office workers.

New York City's two major opera companies – the Metropolitan Opera and the New York City Opera – occupy adjacent buildings at Lincoln Center. If you want to see world-famous artists, go to the Met, but the City Opera also has done some fine work of late. As for classical music concerts, you're likely to find a dozen or so scheduled for a single evening – often at Carnegie Hall (57th Street and 7th Avenue).

You'll have more chances to see good dance performances in New York than in almost any other city in the world, from the American Ballet Theater and New York City Ballet (both at Lincoln Center) to modern dance companies, many of which present their seasons at the Joyce Theater on Eighth Avenue (at 19th Street) and at City Center, on Seventh Avenue (at 55th Street). And one should not forget such notable companies as those of Alvin Ailey, the Dance Theater of Harlem, Merce Cunningham, Pilobolus, and Paul Taylor.

Film

There are hundreds of mainstream movie screens in New York, but here you'll also have the chance to see many films that might not make it to your local multiplex. MOMA QNS, the Walter Reade Theater at Lincoln Center, and the Museum of the Moving Image in Queens all have ongoing film series, mostly revivals of classic and art films. Other places to find movies that you might not otherwise see are: Film Forum (209 West Houston, between 6th Avenue and Varick, tel: 212-727 8110); Lincoln Plaza (Broadway between 62nd and 63rd, tel: 212-757 2280); the Quad Cinema (34 West 13th Street, between 5th and 6th avenues, tel: 212-255 8800); and the Angelika Film Center (Houston and Mercer streets, tel: 212-995 2570). And there are others.

Dance Clubs

The thing to keep in mind is that clubs can be quite different depending on when you go. Some nights are gay, some hetero, some in between. Among the hundreds of ever-changing venues (and themes), you might consider trendy (Serena, 222 West 23rd Street, in the Chelsea Hotel), techno (Metronome, 915 Broadway at 21st Street), mainstream (China Club at 268 West 47th Street), or notorious (CBGB & UMFUG, 315 Bowery at Bleecher Street).

Cabarets and Jazz Clubs

Listen to Jazz at Iridium (1650 Broadway at 51st Street), the Village Vanguard (178 7th Avenue South), the Blue Note (131 West 3rd Street), or Birdland (314 West 44th Street). Some other places where you can hear good music while you drink and/or dine include the Supper Club (240 West 47th Street), Joe's Pub (in the Public Theater, Lafayette Street at Astor Place), or Café Carlyle (35 East 76th Street).

Bars

Hotel bars have made a comeback in New York, and they are now some of the hottest places to go. Most are pretty swank, so bring your gold card. New bars have opened at the Shoreham, Mansfield, and W: The Court hotels. The lobby bars at the Royalton and Four Seasons hotels are fashionable places to meet. Monkey Bar at the Hotel Elysée (60 East 54th Street) and the Paramount Bar in the Paramount Hotel (235 West 46th Street) are old standbys.

Venture to the East Village, and you'll find old-fashioned (McSorley's Old Ale House at 15 East 7th Street), dark (Liquids at 266 East 10th Street), underground (Pravda at 281 Lafayette Street), and fun (Barmacy, 538 East 14th Street).

Greenwich Village offers some brewpubs (Heartland Brewery at 35 Union Square West), the hidden (Chumley's at 80 Bedford Street), and the comfortable (Cedar Tavern at 82 University Place).

Chelsea offers the whole gamut from gay with dancing (Splash at 50 West 17th Street) to gay without attitude (Barracuda at 275 West 22nd Street).

Tried-and-true choices for impromptu celebrations with friends include the Bubble Lounge (228 West Broadway) for champagne, the Rainbow Grill (30 Rockefeller Plaza) for classic cocktails with a sunset view of the city, and the Lenox Lounge (288 Lenox Avenue) for uptown ambiance with jazz.

PLAYING SPORTS

Chances are, you didn't come to New York for the great outdoors, but when New Yorkers want to be active they go to Central Park, where you can hire a bicycle or a boat (both near the Loeb Boathouse, mid-Park near the Bethesda Terrace), a horse (Claremont Stables, 175 West 89th Street, tel: 212-724 5100), or in-line or ice skates (depending on the season, at Wollman Rink, mid-Park at 63rd, or Lasker Rink, 110th and Lenox Avenue). Otherwise, you can just follow the example of the thousands of New Yorkers who jog, bike, and skate in Central Park and along the city pavements. Bowlmor Lanes at 110 University Place in Greenwich Village has 44 bowling lanes and tennis courts upstairs.

Chelsea Piers (23rd Street at the Hudson River) is the one all-purpose destination for all your sporting needs. You'll find facilities for virtually every sport imaginable, including skating, horseback riding and swimming. For a complete run-down, tel: 212-336 6500.

Getting around Central Park

WATCHING SPORTS

Baseball season is roughly from April through September, and NYC has two major-league teams. The Mets play at Shea Stadium in Queens (take the 7 subway right to the stadium), and the Yankees play in the Bronx (the 4 and D subway lines stop at the stadium). You can usually buy tickets at the stadium on game day.

Football season runs from September through January. New York City has no professional football teams, but two play nearby in New Jersey's Meadowlands. The Jets and the Giants both play in Giants Stadium (there's a shuttle-bus service from the Port Authority). Basketball season runs from October through April, and the New York Knicks play at Madison Square Garden at 33rd Street and Seventh Avenue (D, F, R, A, E subways to 34th Street). Tickets are hard to come by, but you can try the box office. Hockey season generally runs from October to April; the New York team is the Rangers, and they play at Madison Square Garden as well. The US Open Tennis championships are played at the US Tennis Center in Queens (7 subway to Shea Stadium) in early September.

Calendar of Events

December 31 New Year's Eve celebration, Times Square.

January Chinese New Year, Chinatown (mid-Jan–mid-Feb).

March St. Patrick's Day Parade, Fifth Avenue (Mar 17).

April Macy's Flower Show (mid-Apr).

May Fleet Week (late May).

June Puerto Rican Day Parade, Fifth Avenue (mid-June). Feast of Sant'Antonio, Sullivan Street, Little Italy (early June). Lesbian and Gay Pride March, Fifth Avenue (late June).

July Independence Day, fireworks on the East River (July 4).

August Harlem Week (2nd week in Aug).

September U.S. Open Tennis, Flushing Meadows, Queens (early Sept). Feast of San Gennaro, Mulberry Street, Little Italy (late Sept).

October New York Film Festival, Lincoln Center (early Oct). Columbus Day Parade, Fifth Avenue (2nd Mon). Greenwich Village Halloween Parade (Oct 31).

November Radio City Music Hall Christmas stage show. New York City Marathon (mid-Nov). Macy's Thanksgiving Day Parade, Broadway (Thanksgiving Day).

December Christmas tree lighting, Rockefeller Center (early Dec).

EATING OUT

New Yorkers dine out a lot, and with over 20,000 restaurants they have plenty of choices. You'll find some of the best restaurants in the country in New York, and some of them are quite expensive. But you won't have to take out a second mortgage on your home to eat well in this city – even in Manhattan. At the most expensive restaurants, it's possible to eat out without spending a fortune (some suggestions on how to save money are offered below). Selected with an eye toward value and staying-power, the list of 'Recommended Restaurants' in the back pages of this guide can help ensure you'll have some fine dining experiences during your visit. But this small selection can't even begin to cover all the top spots in the city. Be aware also that the restaurant scene changes quickly – places come and go with frequency.

Theme restaurants are out. At least that's the conventional wisdom heard around New York nowadays. Some of the most high-profile failures have been the theme restaurants that opened up in the early '90s; the taste for Motown and Hollywood memorabilia and comedy routines served with mediocre and overpriced food seems to have faded, though some old standbys like the Hard Rock Cafe (221 West 57th Street) are still packing the tourists in.

Price

Whenever Wall Street booms, so do expensive restaurants, but the converse effect is also true. The most shocking prices on the menu may be for dessert – it's no longer uncommon to see a $9 price tag – and for water – that bottle of Evian you even didn't realize you were asking for can come also with a $9 price tag (you can always ask for tap water, of course, and even upscale establishments will grant your re-

The Boat Basin Café in Riverside Park, Upper West Side

quest). But even moderately priced restaurants are now feeling more comfortable regularly raising their prices, sometimes annually.

Visitors from California and Europe may be shocked at the cost of wine in New York, where it is not uncommon for restaurateurs to triple or quadruple the retail price of a bottle of wine, raising your favorite $8 bottle of wine to $24, and $14 bottles to almost $50. While this is a common practice in the top tier everywhere, it is common in New York even in the mid-range restaurants. Among expensive restaurants, Union Square Cafe is well known for having a range of good, reasonably priced wines; among the top-tier, Le Cirque 2000 (455 Madison Avenue, 50th/51st) has some relative 'bargains.' In the moderate category, Becco still impresses with a nice selection of wines for under $20. One of the best deals in the city for drinkers is the all-you-can-drink wine dinners at Cité (120 West 51st).

One of the ways to save money at New York's priciest establishments is to drop in for lunch instead of dinner. Lunch is almost always cheaper. For example, a 3-course lunch at Oceana costs $40; for dinner the price tag goes up to $65, even though the quality and variety of the offerings are very similar. *Pre-fix* meals, particularly pre-theater dinners (usually served from 6–7pm) are vastly cheaper than the à la carte menu and are being offered with increasing frequency. Another option is to consider sharing an appetizer or dessert; in some cases, if you inform your waiter that you will be sharing, the kitchen will divide appetizer portions and serve you on separate plates (a good strategy for the ever-present $9 salad served at most expensive restaurants). And be sure to ask for tap water instead of expensive bottled water.

Meals and Meal Times

Breakfast is generally served from 7–9am, though some places open later. Brunch (usually only on weekends) is available from 11am–3pm. Lunch is generally from noon–2pm. Dinner is served any time from 5.30pm until 11, or even later at some spots; unless they are grabbing a quick bite right after work, New Yorkers tend to eat later than residents in most other parts of the US. 'Dinner at 8' still reigns in the top restaurants as the most desirable hour.

Reservations

If you're planning a trip to New York and hope to dine at some of the city's finest restaurants, don't forget to make your dinner reservations along with your hotel reservations, unless you prefer to dine at 5.30 or after 10. Even then, you must book over two weeks in advance for a dinner reservation at Union Square Cafe, and at least one week ahead for a modest but popular place like Blue Water Grill;

If you want an elegant meal but don't want to go out to a restaurant, consider ordering your food by phone. Many top New York restaurants will prepare takeout food, and some will even deliver to your hotel room. Ask your hotel concierge for recommendations.

Grab a bagel

it can take a month to get into a trendy place-of-the-moment. Some of the finest restaurants in New York are not very large. (Of course, if you can't get into Nobu, you can always try your luck standing in line at Next Door Nobu, where reservations aren't accepted).

Dress

Casual dress is fine for most places in New York. Even in a four-star restaurant like Union Square Cafe (21 East 16th Street) you will see diners in shirt-sleeves. There are still a few places (The Four Seasons, 99 East 52nd Street, and Picholine, 35 West 64th Street, for example) that strictly enforce jacket and tie policies. But even places like Patria (250 Park Avenue South, at 20th), which requests 'appropriate' dress, will bend rules. If in doubt, it's best to ask about dress policy when making a reservation.

WHAT AND WHERE TO EAT

Ethnic Enclaves

Chinatown is one of the most famous locales for ethnic dining in New York, but less well known is Flushing, Queens, where you'll find a large variety of very good **Chinese** restaurants. You'll find a group of **Vietnamese** restaurants on Baxter Street, not far from the US Courthouse. Little India, on Sixth Street between First and Second avenues, has a selection of extraordinarily cheap **Indian** restaurants, only a handful of which are actually good (Panna II at 93 1st Avenue, the one with a million chili-pepper lights, is one of the best); another place to look for Indian restaurants is Lexington Avenue in the 20s (Madras Mahal at 104 Lexington Avenue, though inconsistent, has reliably good dosas). **Brazilian** restaurants can be found in a group on 45th and 46th streets in Midtown (between 6th and 7th avenues).

Though little Italy has now shrunk to a couple of blocks of Mulberry Street north of Canal, there are still a few **Italian** restaurants that can pass muster; most of the places here will do if all you want is a plate of pasta and a glass of wine. Another group of Italian restaurants can be found on Bleecker Street in the blocks between Thompson and Seventh Avenue.

For a multi-ethnic feast, look to Ninth Avenue in the 40s and 50s for reasonably priced restaurants of all types.

Dawgs in The East Village

Fast Food

You won't need to resort to Roy Rogers or Pizza Hut Express in Manhattan for a quick lunch or dinner. The following are all reliable inexpensive choices:

The Big Enchilada *160 East 28th Street and 28 East 12th Street*. Fast Mexican food at great prices.

Burritoville *Locations all over Manhattan*. Just what the name suggests; not fancy at all, but quite good.

Così Sandwich Bar *Locations all over Manhattan*. Inventive sandwiches and good lemonade.

Salad bars are not always what they're cracked up to be

Dallas BBQ *132 West 43rd Street, 27 West 72nd Street, 21 University Place, 132 2nd Avenue.* Good, cheap barbecue, if a little greasy.
Daikichi Sushi *20 locations in the city.* Surprisingly good sushi and teriyaki.
Hale and Hearty Soups *Several locations in Midtown.* OK, not the cheapest soup you've ever had, but it's worth the price.

Snacks and Salad

Throughout Manhattan you'll see vendors selling everything from hot dogs to soup to nuts. If you're in a hurry, this food is perfectly good. The same cannot always be said about the so-called serve-yourself 'salad bars' that are found in neighborhood delis all over town. The food is usually put out very early in the morning and kept neither cold enough nor hot enough to inhibit bacterial growth. An average serving also often ends up being more expensive than a sandwich.

New York Specialties

New York is known for pizza, though as anyone who's ever bought a tepid, warmed-over slice from any of the city's myriad pizzerias can tell you, it's not all of the best quality. Stick to John's *(see page 137)*, who will never do you wrong, though you'll have to buy a whole pie – they don't sell single slices.

The same generalization goes for New York hotdogs – they're famous but rarely up to snuff. However, a number of hot dog parlors do excel in this increasingly tight and competitive market, including: the quirky Dawgs on Park at 178 East 7th Street in East Village, with its wide range of specialty dogs; the venerable Papaya King at 179 East 86th Street; and the excellent-value Gray's Papaya (2090 Broadway and 402 6th Avenue).

Bagels were allegedly invented in New York, and the best examples can still be found here; aficionados argue about where the perfect bagel can be found, but you won't go wrong with H&H (2239 Broadway), Ess-a-Bagel (359 1st Avenue or 831 3rd Avenue), or one of the many neighborhood bagel shops. All that can be said for certain is that bagels need to be fresh (no more than a day old), so stick to the shops that make their own; they usually come with cream cheese and sometimes lox (smoked salmon).

Finally, one of New York's specialties isn't a type of food but a place to eat, namely the **coffee shop**. You'll find them dotted all over New York, with vast menus and reasonable prices.

> If you order a 'regular' coffee at a neighborhood deli (not Starbucks), it'll come complete with milk and sugar. In restaurants, you'll be allowed to add your own.

New York's Best

These New York restaurants, though not described

in our 'Restaurants' section, deserve a mention (and a special trip). They are all well worth their high prices for a delicious dining experience. Call in advance for reservations.

Alain Ducasse *In the Essex House Hotel, 155 West 58th Street (6th and 7th avenues), tel: 212-265 7300.* Luxurious and obscenely expensive four-star French cuisine.

Chanterelle *2 Harrison Street (at Hudson), tel: 212-966 6960.* Four-star, Asian-accented cuisine downtown.

Daniel *60 East 65th Street (Madison and Park avenues), tel: 212-288 0033.* Chef Daniel Bouloud's masterpiece.

The Four Seasons *99 East 52nd Street (Lexington and Park avenues), tel: 212-754 9494.* The Grill Room for lunch, the Pool Room for dinner.

Gramercy Tavern *32 East 20th Street (Park and Madison avenues), tel: 212-477 0777.* From the owner of the perennially popular Union Square Café.

Jean-Georges *In the Trump International Hotel, 1 Columbus Circle (60th and 61st streets), tel: 212-299 3900.* Some of New York's most exciting contemporary four-star French cuisine.

Le Cirque 2000 *In the New York Palace Hotel, 455 Madison Avenue (50th and 51st streets), tel: 212-303 7788.* The famous four-star restaurant now in the historic Villard Houses.

Peter Luger Steak House *178 Broadway (Driggs Avenue), Williamsburg, Brooklyn, tel: 718-387 7400.* Take a cab. Perfect porterhouse steak; high prices; no credit cards.

Restaurant Guide

The **Zagat Survey of New York City Restaurants** is one of the best in the Zagat series. Published annually, the book solicits information from frequent diners to produce a compendium that is fairly comprehensive and quite informative. And the same information is now offered on the internet at <www.zagat.com>.

HANDY TRAVEL TIPS

An A–Z Summary of Practical Information

A

ACCOMMODATION (See also YOUTH HOSTELS and YMCAS and the list of RECOMMENDED HOTELS starting on page 125)

Your hotel room will probably be your greatest expense in New York. With more and more tourism and business travel to New York, a decent yet reasonably priced hotel room is becoming increasingly difficult to find. The average price of a hotel room in Manhattan is now about $200 per night. The high season is fall and winter, particularly from late November through New Year's Day, when rates can be as much as 25 percent higher; the low season is January through mid-March, though some hotels also reduce rates in the summer. Advance reservations are important and often crucial; the city is very crowded at all times. And be aware that quoted rates will not include a sales tax of 13.25 percent, plus a $2 per day occupancy tax. Most hotels do not provide breakfast, but there are a few exceptions. At many hotels children can sleep in their parents' room at no extra charge.

AIRPORTS

New York is served by three major airports – **John F. Kennedy International** (JFK) and **Newark International** (EWR), the area's two international airports, and **LaGuardia** (LGA), almost exclusively for domestic flights.

A few recent innovations will make your arrival more pleasant. Luggage carts are now free and available in the baggage claim area. And there are now flat rates for taxis into Manhattan from JFK airport. It is possible to get to and from both LaGuardia and JFK airports via public transportation, but this takes somewhat longer than a cab and is not very convenient if you have lots of luggage. Remember that it is illegal for anyone to approach you offering a taxi service; these touts are unlicensed and not recommended (though you may arrange in advance for a car service to pick you up). Transportation desks inside the terminals offer tickets for various services, including shared minibuses that are cheaper than taxis. For detailed recorded information on transport to and from the airports, call the Port Authority's toll-free number: 1-800-AIR-RIDE (8am–6pm).

For somewhat more than the cost of a taxi, you can book private car service from either LaGuardia or JFK airports. Three recommendable services are Carmel (tel: 212-666 6666), Sabra (tel: 212-777 7171 or 800-722 7122 outside NYC), and Tel Aviv (tel: 212-777 7777 or 800-222 9888 outside NYC). Make your reservation at least 24 hours in advance; a driver will meet you at baggage claim; cost is approximately $30 from LaGuardia, $40 from Kennedy, plus tolls.

John F. Kennedy Airport (tel: 718-244 4444) – Located in Queens, about 15 miles (24 km) from midtown Manhattan; the ride in takes about 45 minutes to an hour, depending on traffic. Taxi: $35 flat rate, not including tolls or tip, to any destination below 96th Street. Shuttle: Gray Line (to major hotels from 5am–7pm), SuperShuttle (to any Manhattan destination 24 hrs), and Carey Transportation (to the Port Authority or its terminal at Park Avenue, between 41st and 42nd streets) all $13–$20. Public Transportation: Free shuttle bus to Howard Beach subway station, then A train (this option usually takes well over an hour but costs only $1.50).

Newark Airport (tel: 201-961 2000) – Located in New Jersey, 16 miles (26 km) from midtown Manhattan; the trip takes 30–45 minutes; Newark is usually more convenient than JFK for those staying in the theater district. Taxi: Not including additions for tolls and crossing the state line ($10 extra) and tip, metered fares usually run around $45. Shuttle: Olympia Trails, approximately $11 to 34th Street/8th Avenue, the Port Authority Bus Terminal on 42nd Street, or an east-side terminal on 41st Street (between 3rd and Lexington). Public Transportation: Difficult and very time-consuming – the trip involves taking a bus to Newark Penn Station, then the PATH train into Manhattan (tel: 800-234-PATH for information); the total cost is $4.

LaGuardia Airport (tel: 718-533 3400) – Located in Queens, 8 miles (13 km) from midtown Manhattan; the ride in takes about 30–40 minutes depending on traffic. Taxi: Not including tolls or tip, usually about $20–$25. Shuttle: Gray Line, SuperShuttle, and Carey – all $10–$16. Public Transport: The M60 bus connects with the subways in Manhattan; Q33, Q47, and Q48 buses connect with the subway in Queens (the trip by subway and bus can take considerably longer than a taxi but still costs only $1.50 if you purchase a MetroCard, which provides free bus-to-subway transfers).

B

BUDGETING FOR YOUR TRIP

To give you an idea of what to expect, here's a list of average prices in US dollars. These prices are only approximate. New York is an expensive city, but it is possible to have a fun vacation on a budget.

Hotels. This will be your major expense. For a double room (before tax), expect to pay up to $150 per night for a budget room, up to $250 a night for a moderate room, up to $350 a night for an expensive room, and over $350 for a luxury room. The only way to spend less than $75 per night is to stay in a hostel or YMCA.

Meals. Breakfast can be had for $5 (more if you sit down in a coffee shop or restaurant); lunch can be as little as $6 for a sandwich and drink from a deli to $10 in an inexpensive restaurant, or more; dinner can cost anywhere from $15 to $150 per person. A glass of wine is rarely less than $5, and a bottle is considered very cheap at $16.

Transportation. An unlimited MetroCard for one week costs $21. It costs about $7 to go across town in a taxi. The amount you pay for airport transfers can be as little as $10 from LaGuardia on a shared mini-bus to $40 from JFK by taxi.

Museums and Attractions. Some museums and attractions are scandalously expensive ($12 for the Guggenheim), but museums belonging to the city (including the Metropolitan Museum of Art, now asking $10) are technically only allowed to ask for a donation, so you can pay as you wish; read the signs carefully. Many museums are free at least one time a week, usually an evening. The Bronx Zoo is free on Wednesday.

C

CAR RENTAL/HIRE (See also DRIVING)

Since New York City has the highest car rental and parking rates in the US (as much as $80 per day), we don't recommend that you rent a car unless you plan to leave the city proper. If you do need a car, though, you'll find that it's generally cheaper to rent one at the airport than in Manhattan, and it's cheaper still to rent a car outside of New York City, where prices are more competitive. We strongly recommend that you make your reservation for car rental before you leave home. (A curious twist on the logic of car rentals is that weekend rentals in Manhattan are more expensive than weekday rentals since most New Yorkers do not own cars and must rent when they go away for the weekend).

You will need a major credit card to rent a car (or you must be willing to put up a very hefty cash deposit). The minimum age for renting a car is 21, but some companies will not rent to drivers under 25, or when they do will impose a high additional fee.

CHILDREN'S ACTIVITIES

Virtually all of New York City's museums have programs or offerings for children, but the Children's Museum of Manhattan *(see page 63)* is devoted entirely to their interests. Young visitors also enjoy the playgrounds dotting Central Park. The New Victory Theater is primarily devoted to children's theater, though grade-schoolers also enjoy many

Broadway musicals. Many local bookstores have children's story hours. Kids generally enjoy the double-decker bus tours of the city and the boat rides (as long as they aren't too long). In short, you will have no trouble finding interesting things to do if you have kids in tow.

CLIMATE

Summers (mid-June to early September) in New York are hot and humid; winters (mid-November to early March) are generally cold. Spring (early April to mid-June) and fall (mid-September to mid-November) have the best weather. Air-conditioning is available almost everywhere, even on subway trains.

Here are monthly average maximum and minimum daytime temperatures:

	J	F	M	A	M	J	J	A	S	O	N	D
°F	39	40	48	61	71	81	85	83	77	67	54	41
	26	27	34	44	53	63	68	66	60	51	41	30
°C	7	4	9	16	22	27	29	28	25	19	12	5
	3	3	1	7	12	17	20	19	15	10	5	1

CLOTHING

Casual dress is acceptable in most places, even at the theater, though some more expensive restaurants will require a jacket and tie for men. In the summer, light clothing made of natural fibers is recommended because of the hot and sticky climate.

COMPLAINTS

First, try to address your complaint to the establishment. If you feel you have reason to complain about retail stores or business practices, you should contact the New York City Department of Consumer Affairs: 42 Broadway, New York, NY 10013, tel: 212-487 8398 or 487 4444. To complain about taxi drivers or fares, *see pages 119–21.*

CRIME (See also EMERGENCIES)

While New York is the safest major city in the US, petty theft is still common, especially pick-pocketing at crowded intersections and subway train entrances. By taking a few simple precautions, however, you can increase your safety:

● Always lock your hotel room door, and never admit any unauthorized person.

● Deposit valuables in the in-room or hotel safe.

● Never carry large amounts of cash; wear a minimum of jewelry (gold neck chains are especially targeted items).

● Carry as much money as possible in the form of traveler's checks, and keep a record of these (and your passport) separate from the checks, or simply use your ATM card, withdrawing only as much cash as you'll need for the day.

● Never leave valuables (bags, etc). unattended or behind your back even for a few seconds, and don't leave bags draped over the chair in a restaurant (place them between your feet).

● If you are robbed, don't play the hero – hand over what you have. Then report it to the police immediately (tel: 646-610 5000 or 911 for emergencies): your insurance company will need to see a copy of the police report (as may your consulate if your passport is stolen). For stolen or lost traveler's checks and credit cards, report the matter at once to the issuer so that they can be stopped immediately.

CUSTOMS AND ENTRY REQUIREMENTS (See also AIRPORTS)

Canadians need only provide evidence of their nationality. Citizens of the UK, Australia, New Zealand, and the Republic of Ireland no longer need a visa for stays of less than 90 days, but only a valid passport and a return airline ticket. The airline will issue a visa waiver form. Citizens of South Africa need a visa – check with your local US consulate or embassy and allow three weeks for delivery.

Duty-free allowance: you will be asked to complete a customs declaration form before you arrive in the US. Restrictions are as follows:

you are generally allowed to bring in a reasonable quantity of tobacco and alcohol for your personal use. A non-resident may claim, free of duty and taxes, articles up to $100 in value for use as gifts for other persons. The exemption is valid only if the gifts accompany you, you stay 72 hours or more, and have not claimed this exemption within the preceding six months. Up to 100 cigars may be included within this gift exemption (Cuban cigars, however, are forbidden and may be confiscated). Arriving and departing passengers must report any money or checks, etc., exceeding a total of $10,000.

D

DRIVING (See also CAR RENTAL/HIRE)

Driving conditions. Visitors arriving by car would do well to leave their vehicle parked in a garage and use public transportation, as traffic and scarce parking space make driving a nightmare. If you must drive, remember certain rules: the speed limit is 30 mph (50 km/h) unless otherwise indicated; you may not (legally) use your horn in the city; the use of seat belts is mandatory; the speed limit on most highways in the city is 55 mph (90 km/h) and strictly enforced – look for signs, as on some major highways it has been raised to 65 mph (105 km/h) and, of course, visitors must remember to drive on the right.

Before leaving home, determine whether your own insurance will cover you when you're driving a rented car; if it does, you won't need to take out car rental insurance.

Parking. While street parking is possible in some areas outside of Midtown, a garage or parking lot is the safer though far more expensive choice. If you happen to find a parking spot on the street, obey posted parking regulations, which may include parking only on one side of the street on alternate days. Never park next to a fire hydrant and don't leave your car over the time limit, or it may be towed away.

Gas (petrol). Service stations are few and far between in the city (11th and 12th avenues on the West Side are good hunting grounds). They are often open in the evening and on Sundays.

Breakdowns and insurance. The Automobile Club of New York (ACNY), a branch of the American Automobile Association (AAA), will help members as well as foreign visitors affiliated with other recognized automobile associations. In case of a breakdown, or for other problems along the way, call their Emergency Road Service (tel: 800-222 4357) or wait until a police car comes along.

Automobile Club of New York: Broadway and 62nd Street, New York, NY 10023, tel: (212)-586-1166; web site: <www.aaa.com>.

E

ELECTRICITY

110-volt 60-cycle AC is standard throughout the US. Plugs are the flat, parallel two-pronged variety. Foreign visitors without dual-voltage appliances will need a transformer and adapter plug.

EMBASSIES AND CONSULATES

Embassies are located in Washington, DC, but most countries have consulates or missions to the United Nations in New York.
Australia: Consulate General, 150 East 42nd Street, tel: (212) 351 6500
Canada: 1251 Avenue of the Americas, tel: (212) 596 1628
Republic of Ireland: 345 Park Avenue, tel: (212) 319 2555
New Zealand: 780 3rd Avenue, tel: (212) 832 4038
South Africa: 333 E. 38th Street, tel: (212) 213 4880
United Kingdom: 845 Third Avenue, tel: (212) 745 0200

EMERGENCIES (See also HEALTH & MEDICAL CARE AND POLICE)

All-purpose emergency number: 911

G

GAY AND LESBIAN TRAVELERS

New York has a sizable gay and lesbian population. While Greenwich Village, especially Christopher Street, is still a center for gay life (you'll find The Monster and other bars here), Chelsea is now the more fashionable gay neighborhood, where many gay restaurants and shops can be found (especially along 8th Avenue from 14th to 23rd streets). For gay events and nightlife information, consult *Time Out New York*.

GETTING THERE

Getting to New York by air is a fairly simple proposition. Most airlines have several flights a day to one of New York's airports. Newark is a major hub for Continental Airlines; from Australia and New Zealand, it is served by Qantas and United; from Europe by British Airways, American, and Virgin Atlantic; and from Canada by Air Canada. Other airlines with flights into Newark include American, Delta, Northwest, many with international connections. JFK is a major hub for Air France, American, British Air, and Virgin Atlantic; connections to any European airline are quite good, as are connections to Canada via Air Canada, and other carriers, and to Asia and the Pacific via Cathay Pacific. LaGuardia, which serves mostly domestic flights, is a major hub of USAir, Delta, and American; Continental-and United also fly to and from LaGuardia, as does Air Canada.

GUIDES AND TOURS

A good way to get started in New York is to take advantage of one of the double-decker hop-on-hop-off bus tours. There are a few operators, and they all go to all the top tourist spots. Numerous companies offer a variety of organized tours (walking tours, helicopter, nightclub rounds, historical tours, etc). Individual guides are also available. See 'What to Do' *(page 83)* for more information. You can also check the Friday and Sunday *New York Times* (Arts section) or *Time*

Out New York, or contact NYC & Company *(see page 122)* for the names of reputable tour operators.

H

HEALTH AND MEDICAL CARE

The US has a very good though expensive health-care system, and New York has many of the country's top hospitals. Payment for any medical services will be expected on the spot. It is wise to arrange for health and accident insurance during your trip before your visit, either through your travel agency or an insurance company. In an emergency, your hotel should be able to provide a list of doctors.

Pharmacies. It is generally advisable to bring with you any medicines you require regularly. Be aware that many medicines you can buy over the counter in your home country require a prescription in the US. If you need prescription drugs during your stay, you will have to get a prescription from a local physician. CVS has a 24-hour pharmacy for prescrition needs at 2nd Avenue and 72nd Street, tel: 212-249 5699.

HOLIDAYS

The following are national holidays in the US. In New York City, banks, offices, and some stores and museums are closed on these days:

New Year's Day	January 1
Martin Luther King Day	Third Monday in January
President's Day	Third Monday in February
Memorial Day	Last Monday in May
Independence Day	July 4
Labor Day	First Monday in September
Columbus Day	Second Monday in October
Veterans' Day	November 11
Thanksgiving Day	Fourth Thursday in November
Christmas Day	December 25

L

LAUNDRY AND DRY CLEANING

Self-service laundries are located throughout the city; ask at your hotel – some even have self-service facilities on-site. Dry-cleaners are also widely available and reasonably priced.

LOST PROPERTY

Each transport system maintains its own lost property office. Here are two useful numbers:

New York City Transit Authority (NYCTA, subway network and bus system) Lost Property Office: tel: (212) 424 4343.

NYC Taxi and Limousine Commission Lost Property: tel: (212) 692 8294.

M

MEDIA

Radio and Television. Almost all New York City hotel rooms have cable television, including CNN. Channel 1 on Time-Warner cable systems is a 24-hour station devoted to local news, weather, and events. There are about 50 local AM and FM radio stations operating in the New York area.

Magazines and Newspapers. The city's major English-language daily newspapers are the *Daily News*, *New York Times*, and *New York Post*. Newsstands are prevalent in all the boroughs. You can also find newspapers in almost any language imaginable. Several local weeklies, including *The New Yorker*, *New York*, and *Time Out New York* have information about goings on about town. The *Village Voice*, also weekly, is free.

MONEY

Currency. The dollar is divided into 100 cents. The coins are as follows: 1¢ (penny), 5¢ (nickel), 10¢ (dime), 25¢ (quarter), and $1 (new in 2000). Bank notes of $1, $5, $10, $20, $50 and $100 are common, but some establishments will not accept denominations over $20 unless you make an especially large purchase.

Credit cards. The major cards are widely accepted, sometimes even at movie theaters. (One place where you will not be able to use a credit card, however, is the TKTS reduced-price ticket booth, where only cash or traveler's checks are accepted).

Exchange facilities. Most banks are open weekdays from 9am–3pm (often till 6pm on Thursday) and many are open Saturday as well. Currency exchange offices at the airports remain open at the weekend. Branches of the Chase Manhattan Bank, Citibank, and the bigger offices of other major banks change foreign currency and foreign traveler's checks. There are a few private currency exchange bureaus in tourist areas, and you may be able to change money at your hotel, though you probably won't get the best rate at either. Or use your ATM card.

ATMs. These are widely available. However, most banks charge non-depositors a small fee to use their ATMs.

Sales tax. There is no VAT in the US, so sales tax of 8¼ percent is added to the price of all goods purchased in New York City, including meals in restaurants and to certain food items. Clothing items under $110 are tax-free.

Traveler's checks. It is wise to buy traveler's checks denominated in US$. Foreign currency traveler's checks must be exchanged at a bank.

O

OPEN HOURS

Banks. Mon–Fri 9am–3pm, some open until 4pm; many open Sat 9am–2pm.

Offices. 9am–5pm is the norm.

Stores. Most stores are open Mon–Sat 10am–6pm.

Restaurants. Many New Yorkers dine late, so many restaurants are open until at least 11pm during the week, and until midnight or later on Friday and Saturday.

ORIENTATION

Getting your bearings in Manhattan is remarkably easy. Apart from Lower Manhattan, where the thoroughfares twist and turn, and may even be named, all the straight thoroughfares running from west to east are called 'streets' and are numbered from south to north (1st, 2nd, 3rd, etc). In addresses, the addition of a 'West' (W) or an 'East' (E) after the address number show whether it lies to the west or east of Fifth Avenue.

The avenues run north-south, intersecting with the streets at right angles. They too are numbered, from (starting in the east) First to Twelfth Avenue. Some have their own names, such as York Avenue, Lexington Avenue, Park Avenue and Madison Avenue; and Sixth Avenue is officially called Avenue of the Americas. There's just one street that doesn't conform to this pattern: Broadway cuts across the island diagonally.

P

PHOTOGRAPHY AND VIDEO

All popular brands of film and photographic equipment are available. Pre-recorded videotapes bought in the US will not work in Europe. Tapes can be converted, but at considerable expense.

POLICE (See also CRIME AND EMERGENCIES)

In an emergency, dial 911. The New York police department is highly visible: on foot, horseback, bicycles, and in cars. You will also see them patrolling the subway.

POST OFFICES

The US Post Office only deals with mail. Branches are generally open weekdays from 8am–5pm and on Saturday from 9am–1pm. New York's General Post Office (421 8th Avenue, New York, NY 10001), stays open 24 hours. A domestic letter costs 37¢, a domestic postcard 23¢; a postcard sent overseas costs 70¢, an overseas aerogram 80¢. You can often buy stamps at the reception desk in your hotel, in many grocery stores, or from stamp machines, though these may cost more than at the post office. Mailboxes are painted blue and are numerous in Manhattan, less so in other boroughs.

PUBLIC TRANSPORTATION (See also AIRPORTS)

Virtually every place in New York City that visitors are likely to go can be reached by public transportation. The flat fare is $2 (for bus or subway) one-way. If you purchase a MetroCard, you can transfer between buses and subways for free. In addition to paying for each ride, you may buy an unlimited daily ($7) or weekly ($21) MetroCard. MetroCards, including the daily FunPass, can be purchased at all subway stations and at many drug and grocery stores and newsstands, including some supermarkets. Bus and subway maps are available at major subway stations and transit hubs. For directions to reach any address in New York City by public transportation, tel: (718) 330 1234. Information is also available online at <www.mta.nyc.ny.us>.

Buses. All public buses are numbered and for Manhattan bear the prefix M (Q for Queens, B for Brooklyn, and Bx for the Bronx). Most either follow the avenues (except Park Avenue) or run cross-town along the major two-way arteries. They accept only exact fare (or a token or a MetroCard). Bus stops are indicated by a signpost showing a blue-and-white bus logo, and the bus number. Enter by the front door, pay your fare, and leave via the rear door. MetroCard users can transfer from bus to subway for free.

Subway. It operates 24 hours a day, but not all subway entrances and token booths are open at all times. You may wish to avoid peak times (7–9.30am and 4.30–7pm). It is generally possible to make free transfers from one subway line to another at major transfer points. Local trains make every stop on the line; express trains may not. Lines are color-coded and identified by the stations at the end of the lines. Make sure you know the direction you're traveling in: *downtown* is southwards, *uptown* northwards.

Despite occasional incidents, the subway is very safe: 3½ million New Yorkers ride it every day, and on many lines in Manhattan, you'll see as many people on the train at 2am as you will at 2pm.

Commuter Rail Lines. The Long Island Railroad provides rail service from Penn Station at 33rd Street and Seventh Avenue between Manhattan and Long Island (tel: 516-822 LIRR in Long Island and 718-217 LIRR in New York City). The Metro-North commuter railroad provides rail service between Manhattan and counties to the north of New York, including southwest Connecticut (tel: 800-METRO-INFO outside NYC and 212-532 4900 within NYC). PATH trains go from 33rd Street and Sixth Avenue to New Jersey (fare is $1 payable in exact change as you enter the station).

Taxis. Taxis are painted yellow and metered. If the light on top is lit, the cab is available. In Manhattan you can easily hail a taxi on the street, or go to a major hotel's taxi stand. Every taxi driver is expected to be able to speak English and to be able to take you to any address in New York City; they cannot legally refuse a fare if you are going to a destination within the city limits. The meter starts at $2.50 and increases by 30¢ every ⅕-mile (or 20¢ for waiting time). There is a 50¢ surcharge from 8pm–6am. If your route comprises a toll tunnel or bridge, you must pay the toll. Taxi drivers will not accept bills higher than $20. Drivers generally expect a tip (about 15 percent or round up to the nearest dollar). To complain about a driver, note his or her name and number and contact the NYC Taxi and Limousine Commission (tel: 212-221 8294). Such complaints are taken seriously.

T

TELEPHONE/FAX

Telephones. You can dial directory assistance (number 411) or an operator (dial 0) for free from any New York City payphone. All numbers with an 800, 888, or 877 prefix are toll-free. For domestic long-distance calls in the US, dial 1 + the area code + the 7-digit number. For international calls, dial 011 + the country code + the number.

New York has five area codes: 212 and 646 for Manhattan; 917 primarily for cell phones and pagers, but also for Manhattan; 718 and 347 for the Bronx, Queens, Brooklyn, and Staten Island. If you are calling a number outside of the area code you are in you must first dial 1 + the area code + the 7-digit number (though you will be charged only for a local call).

Local calls cost 25¢ for the first three minutes, after which the operator will tell you to add more money. Most newsstands and drug stores sell calling cards for long-distance calls. You may wish to avoid the hefty surcharges hotels add to all outgoing calls by using a calling card and a payphone.

Fax. You can send a fax (expensively) from almost any New York City hotel. But you can also send a fax (much less expensively) from a Mailboxes Etc. or Kinko's, both of which have outlets throughout the city.

TIME ZONES

New York City is on Eastern Standard Time. In summer (between April and October) Daylight Saving Time is adopted and clocks move ahead one hour. The chart below shows the time in various cities in winter:

Los Angeles	**New York**	London	Paris	Sydney
9am	noon	5pm	6pm	4am

TIPPING

Service is never included in restaurant prices, but it is sometimes added to the bill (your receipt must clearly say if the service has been added to the bill). In a restaurant, tip 15 percent (New Yorkers traditionally double the 8¼ percent tax). In general, porters are tipped $1 per bag; cloakroom attendants and doormen who find you a taxi, $1; taxi drivers and hairdressers, 15–20 percent.

TOILETS

Clean public toilets are hard to come by in Manhattan. In general, the best facilities are those in the lobbies of major hotels or in department stores. Good bets in the Times Square area are the Marriott Marquis, the Virgin Megastore, and the Times Square Visitor Center; in Lower Manhattan, the Museum of the American Indian; in Greenwich Village, the Virgin Megastore on Union Square. There are also public toilets in Washington Square Park (but don't use them at night). Restaurants usually want you to buy something in order to give you access to their facilities; you could also try one of the numerous Starbucks or McDonald's, where buying something isn't such a burden on your wallet and where the toilets are usually decent.

TOURIST INFORMATION

NYC & Company is a non-profit organization subsidized by the city's hotels and merchants. The staff at their office and gift shop provides maps and leaflets about tourist attractions, a price list of major hotels, and other info: 810 Seventh Avenue (52nd and 53rd streets), tel: (212) 484 1222. Open Mon–Fri 8.30am–6pm, Sat–Sun 9am–5pm. There are two additional NYC & Company kiosks located at City Hall Park downtown and 125th Street and Adam Clayton Powell Boulevard in Harlem.

A visitor center operated by the Times Square Business Improvement District is located in the Embassy Theater at 1560 Broadway (46th and 47th streets); you'll be able to get cash (through Fleet Bank ATMs), buy theater tickets (for a fee), and get information on every attraction in New York, plus connect to the Internet for free. You can also buy a Metrocard FunPass here.

TRAVELERS WITH DISABILITIES

Most New York street corners are graded for wheelchairs. Buses can accommodate wheelchairs, though most subway stations are not accessible. Many hotels have rooms for guests with disabilities, but check when you make your reservation because some older establishments do not. The Mayor's Office for People with Disabilities (52 Chambers Street, Room 206, New York, NY 10007, tel: 212-788 2830) can provide further information.

W

WEBSITES

Several websites will prove useful information when you are planning your trip: CitySearch <www.newyork.citysearch.com> has fairly comprehensive coverage of everything in the city, including restaurant reviews. NYC & Company <www.nycvisit.com> has some useful information but sends you to CitySearch for most of the details. *Time Out New York* <www.timeoutnewyork.com> has useful coverage of events, as well as some information on bars and restaurants. The Metropolitan Transportation Authority <www.mta.nyc.ny.us> has a very comprehensive website listing regional transportation options.

Here are the websites of some of the main attractions:
American Museum of Natural History <www.amnh.org>.
Empire State Building <www.esbnyc.com>.
The Frick Collection <www.frick.org>
Solomon R Guggenheim Museum <www.guggenheim.org>.
The Intrepid Sea-Air-Space Museum <www.intrepid-museum.com>.
The Jewish Museum <www.jewishmuseum.org>.
The Metropolitan Museum of Art <www.metmuseum.org>.
Museum of the City of New York <www.mcny.org>.
The Museum of Modern Art (MOMA) <www.moma.org>
The National Museum of the American Indian <www.si.edu/nmai>.
South Street Seaport Museum <www.southstseaport.org>.
Statue of Liberty/Ellis Island <www.nps.gov>.
Whitney Museum of American Art <www.whitney.org>.

WEIGHTS AND MEASURES

The US is one of the few countries in the world that doesn't use the
metric system.

Y

YOUTH HOSTELS AND YMCAs (See also ACCOMMODATIONS)

The New York International AYH-Hostel is located at 891 Amsterdam
Avenue, NYC 10025 (tel: 212-932 2300; fax 212-932 2574). There
are also two YMCAs, where you can have a single or shared room with
access to shared baths on a sex-segregated floor with exercise facilities: the Vanderbilt YMCA, 224 East 47th Street, NYC 10017 (tel: 212-
755 2410); and the West Side YMCA, 5 West 63rd Street, NYC 10023
(tel: 212-787 4400; fax 212-875 1334).

There are also a number of other private hostels and hotels with dorms,
including the Gershwin Hotel. Another reasonably priced alternative for
rooms can be found through the Bed and Breakfast Network of NY Inc,
tel: 212-645 8134.

Recommended Hotels

The only way to beat New York's notoriously high hotel rates is to come during the off-season (roughly January to March) or to get a package deal or weekend special. Advance reservations are essential most of the year. You'll find the highest concentration of hotels in Midtown, between 42nd and 59th streets; others are in the 30s, both on the west side (near Herald Square) and on the east side (Murray Hill, including Gramercy Park). What you will not find here are most of the $400-plus luxury hotels, as these are out of the reach of most people.

Inquire direct about weekend specials; otherwise there are several US reservation services offering discounts of 50 percent or more on upscale rooms. Try the online service at: <www.hoteldiscount.com>.

The following categories apply to the cost of a standard or superior double room for one night and do not include tax of 13.5 percent plus $2 per room. Unless otherwise indicated, rooms have private baths, direct-dial phones, cable television, and air-conditioning.

$$$$$	over $400
$$$$	$300–$400
$$$	$200–$300
$$	$150–$200
$	below $150

MIDTOWN

The Benjamin $$$$ *125 East 50th Street (at Lexington Avenue,) NYC 10022, tel: (212) 715-2500 or (888) 423-6526; fax: (212) 715-2525; <www.mesuite.com>.* One of NYC's newest boutique business hotels, the Benjamin offers four-star amenities and some of the most comfortable beds in New York at relatively reasonable prices. Rooms have galley or full kitchens, some have terraces. The building was erected in 1927, and created by world-renowned architect Emery Roth. 209 rooms.

Casablanca Hotel $$$ *147 West 43rd Street (6th Avenue and Broadway), NYC 10036, tel: (212) 869-1212 or (888) 922-7225; fax: (212) 391-7585; <www.casablancahotel.com>.* Wonderful, small hotels are rare in New York, yet here is a lovely and inviting choice. The décor throughout evokes Morocco, with Murano glass hallway sconces and beautifully tiled and appointed bathrooms. Continental breakfast included. 48 rooms.

Edison Hotel $$ *228 West 47th Street (Broadway and 8th Avenue), NYC 10036, tel: (212) 840-5000 or (800) 637-7070; fax: (212) 596-6850; <www.edisonhotelnyc.com>.* Hotels in the bottom price ranges hardly ever really stand out here, but the Edison is an exception. Though the Art Deco lobby can be chaotic, the rooms in this huge hotel are quite comfortable, pleasantly if simply decorated, and quiet. May be the best deal in NYC. 1,000 rooms.

Four Seasons Hotel New York $$$$$ *57 East 57th Street (Park and Madison avenues), NYC 10022, tel: (212) 758-5700 or (800) 819-5030; fax: (212) 758-5711; <www.fourseasons.com>.* Arguably New York's best hotel, the Four Seasons has some of the largest rooms in the city (along with some of the highest prices). Elegant features include blond wood furnishings, bedside controls for everything, and separate showers and tubs. The restaurant, Fifty Seven Fifty Seven, and the lobby bar are also top-notch. 370 rooms.

Hotel Iroquois $$$ *49 West 44th Street (5th and 6th avenues), NYC 10036, tel: (212) 840-3080 or (800) 332-7220; fax: (212) 398-1754; <www.iroquoisny.com>.* This luxurious boutique hotel is close enough to the theater district to be convenient but far enough away to be out of the path of most of the crowds. Standard rooms are not large, but they accommodate a king-size bed without feeling too cramped. The health club is first-rate. 114 rooms.

Mansfield $$$–$$$$ *12 West 44th Street (5th and 6th avenues), NYC 10019, tel: (212) 944-6050 or (800) 255-5167; fax: (212) 764-4477; <www.mansfieldhotel.com>.* A carefully restored Edwardian gem, this hotel is situated off the crush of Times Square. The only drawback is that standard rooms are small and lack real closets. Suites, however, are sumptuous. The lobby bar is a great place for a quiet drink. Continental breakfast included. 124 rooms.

Millennium Broadway $$$$ *145 West 44th Street (6th Avenue and Broadway), NYC 10036, tel: (212) 768-4400 or (800) 622-5569; fax: (212) 768-0847; <www.millenniumbroadway.com>*. All of the rooms in this modern neoclassic tower are large and tastefully appointed, and all feature the usual business hotel amenities (two-line phones with dataports, desks, and, in Club Rooms, fax machines). 629 rooms; 125 premier rooms.

Paramount Hotel $$–$$$ *235 West 46th Street (8th Avenue and Broadway), NYC 10036, tel: (212) 764-5500 or (800) 225-7474; fax: (212) 354-5237; <www.paramounthotelnewyork.com>*. Designed by Philippe Starck, style virtually oozes from every black-clad pore of this Theater District hotel just steps from Times Square, but some of the rooms are so small you feel you have to take a deep breath to turn around. On the plus side, each room has a VCR, and there is a good health club. 601 rooms.

Portland Square Hotel $ *132 West 47th Street (6th and 7th avenues), NYC 10036, tel: (212) 382-0600 or (800) 388-8988; fax: 382-0684; <www.portlandsquarehotel.com>*. This budget hotel is a sister property of the Herald Square Hotel. Rooms are not large, and service and amenities are minimal, but for the price, this isn't a bad choice. 113 rooms, some with shared bathrooms.

The Roosevelt $$$ *Madison Avenue (at 45th Street), NYC 10017, tel: (212) 661-9600 or (800) 223-1870; fax: (800) 661-4475; email: <nyrsales@attmail.com>*. This large hotel near Grand Central Terminal has recently been massively renovated. Rooms are traditionally decorated. Popular with tour groups, it's a good base from which to explore the city if you don't want to be in the Times Square area. 1,040 rooms.

The Royalton $$$$ *44 West 44th Street (5th and 6th avenues), NYC 10036, tel: (212) 869-4400; fax: 869-8965*. To be hired by the Royalton, prospective staff members must bring a head shot to the interview, which may give you some idea of what this trendy hotel is like. But it's still always a shock to walk into the dark, royal-blue hallways. Rooms here are lavishly designed for style without, as in so many cases, compromising the comfort. It's a great place to meet friends for lunch at the hotel's Restaurant 44, or for a drink in the ultra-hip lobby bar. 205 rooms.

The Shoreham $$$$ *33 West 55th Street (5th and 6th avenues), NYC 10019, tel: (212) 247-6700 or (800) 553-3347; fax: (212) 765-9741; <www.shorehamhotel.com>.* On a quiet residential street just around the corner from the (temporarily closed) Museum of Modern Art. A 1999 renovation added a sleek lobby and bar and doubled the hotel's guest rooms. Rooms are fairly small but sumptuous and comfortable. La Caravalle, a great New York dining institution, is located downstairs. 176 rooms.

HERALD SQ., MURRAY HILL, GRAMERCY PARK

Hotel Bedford $$ *118 East 40th Street (Park and Lexington avenues), NYC 10016, tel: (212) 697-4800 or (800) 221-6881; fax: (212) 697-1093; email: <bedford@cosmoweb.net>.* What sets this unpretentious hotel apart are its friendly staff and personalized service. The rooms and public areas are well-kept. Located on a quiet block near Grand Central Terminal, continental breakfast is included. 78 rooms, 58 suites.

Deauville Hotel $ *103 East 29th Street (Park and Lexington avenues), NYC 10016, tel: (212) 683-0990 or (800) 333-8843; fax: (212) 689-5921.* This inexpensive hotel is popular with budget travelers (small rooms with shared bath go for as little as $80), but it's a good location for anyone looking for a clean and simple room. The attractive building was recently remodeled, and the friendly staff make you feel right at home. 58 rooms.

Gershwin $ *7 East 27th Street (5th and Madison avenues), NYC 10016, tel: (212) 545-8000; fax: (212) 684-5546; <www.gershwin-hotel.com>.* A fun, youth-oriented budget hotel, where rooms and hallways feature the work of contemporary artists. 'Superior' rooms are spare but stylishly decorated and not too small; expect less in 'standard' and 'economy'. 106 rooms.

Gramercy Park Hotel $$ *2 Lexington Avenue (at 21st Street), NYC 10010, tel: (212) 475-4320 or (800) 221-4083; fax: (212) 505-0535.* Whatever grandeur this hotel once had is faded now, though the renovated rooms aren't as frayed and gloomy as they used to be. Most have been nicely redone and offer basic and comfortable lodgings at a reasonable price. The location near Gramercy Park and all the wonderful restaurants on lower Park Avenue are hard to beat. 507 rooms.

Herald Square Hotel $ *19 West 31st Street (5th Avenue and Broadway), NYC 10001, tel: (212) 279-4017 or (800) 727-1888; fax: (212) 643-9208; <www.heraldsquarehotel.com>.* The former *Life* magazine headquarters is now a budget hotel popular with international travelers. While some of the rooms are dark, they're not too small (except for the singles) and are decently furnished and clean. 135 rooms, 11 with shared baths.

Hotel Metro $$–$$$ *45 West 35th Street (5th and 6th avenues), NYC 10001, tel: (212) 947-2500; fax: (212) 279-1310;<www. hotelmetronyc.com>.* The lovely Art Deco lobby, with fresh flowers and leather chairs, is an oasis from gritty 35th Street. Guest rooms are fairly large and meticulously clean; the family suites are a good choice, offering two separate sleeping areas for less than the price of two rooms. Great value. 177 rooms.

Ramada Inn Eastside $ *161 Lexington Avenue (at 30th Street), NYC 10016, tel: (212) 545-1800 or (800) 567-7720; fax: (212) 481-7270.* Reasonable prices and nice rooms make this small Murray Hill hotel a real find. Nicely decorated, colonial-style rooms. Good Indian restaurants nearby on Lexington Avenue. Continental breakfast included. 96 rooms.

Roger Williams Hotel $$$ *131 Madison Avenue (at 31st Street), NYC 10016, tel: (212) 448-7000 or (877) 847-4444; fax: (212) 448-7007; <www.rogerwilliamshotel.com>.* This boutique hotel near Madison Square Park and the Flatiron Building, with a soaring lobby and soothing rooms, appeals to travelers who look for style with their room. Shoji screens cover the windows in nice-sized rooms, and little extras like CD players, VCRs, and a work desk make this a very attractive choice in Murray Hill. Continental breakfast included. 181 rooms.

Shelburne Murray Hill $$$–$$$$ *303 Lexington Avenue (at 37th Street), NYC 10016, tel: (212) 320-8025 or (800) ME-SUITE; fax: (212) 779-7068; <www.mesuite.com>.* Renovated in 1999, the traditionally styled Shelburne offers good-sized suites with colonial-style furnishings, pull-out couches, and kitchens. A good choice for families and business travelers. Health club. 263 rooms.

W New York: The Court $$$$ *130 East 39th Street (at Lexington Avenue), NYC 10016, tel: (212) 685-1100; fax: (212) 889-0287; <www.starwood.com>.* One of the newest in Starwood's chain of high-tech, upscale business hotels, the Court has never looked better. The large rooms have all the trimmings you would expect at these prices, including Web TV and internet access with a cordless keyboard. 198 rooms, 40 suites. A few doors down, W New York: The Tuscany (120 East 39th Street, tel: 212/686-1600; fax: 212/779-7822), has 122 slightly larger rooms and 12 suites at slightly higher prices.

Hotel Wolcott $–$$ *4 West 31st Street (5th Avenue and Broadway), NYC 10001, tel: (212) 268-2900; fax: (212) 563-0096; <www.wolcott.com>.* The gilded (though faded) lobby in this reasonably priced hotel is an attractive holdover from the Edith Wharton age. A standout in its price category. Rooms come with either one, two, or three beds and are well-kept and clean. Small fitness center. 163 rooms.

DOWNTOWN

Best Western Seaport Inn $$ *33 Peck Slip, NYC 10038, tel: (212) 766 6600 or (800) HOTEL-NY; fax: (212) 766 6615; <www.bestwestern.com>.* A block from South Street Seaport, this converted 19th-century warehouse features antiques and more modern amenitites like vCRs and mini-fridges. Some rooms on the upper floors have Jacuzzis and/or terraces with views of the Brooklyn Bridge. 72 rooms.

Holiday Inn Downtown $$$ *138 Lafayette Street, NYC 10013, tel: (212) 966-8898 or (800) 465-4329; fax: (212) 966-3933; <www.holiday-inn.com>.* This remodeled period hotel is only a block from Chinatown and very convenient to the galleries and shops of Soho. The rooms aren't terribly large, but the hotel does offer the usual Holiday Inn amenities, and that's not a bad thing at all. 227 rooms.

Mercer Hotel $$$$ *147 Mercer Street, NYC 10013, tel: (212) 966-6060 or (888) 918-6060; fax: (212) 965-3838; <www. mercerhotel.com>.* A converted 1890s landmark building in the heart of Soho, the rooms feature high loft ceilings, arched windows, and (for New York) spacious bath facilities. Expect a stylish clientele and great food from the acclaimed Mercer Kitchen restaurant. 75 rooms.

Soho Grand Hotel $$$$–$$$$$ *310 West Broadway, NYC 10013, tel: (212) 965-3000; fax: (212) 965-3244; <www.sohogrand.com>.* A sophisticated but comfortable hotel with all the high-tech and stylish amenties you might expect from an upscale hostelry that caters to the media and music-biz crowds. As befits a place owned by the heir to the Hartz Mountain pet empire, pets are welcome; for anyone who arrives without an animal companion, the management may be able to provide a complimentary bowl of goldfish. 369 rooms.

Washington Square Hotel $ *103 Waverly Place (MacDougal Street and 6th Avenue), NYC 10011, tel: (212) 777-9515 or (800) 222-0418; fax: (212) 979-8373; <www.wshotel.com>.* This small, European-style hotel in Greenwich Village is one of the few inexpensive options downtown. Guest rooms, some of which look out over the park, are brightly decorated, and the restaurant, C3, is one of the neighborhood's hidden secrets. 170 rooms.

THE UPPER EAST SIDE

The Franklin $$$ *164 East 87th Street (3rd and Lexington avenues), NYC 10128, tel: (212) 355-0100 or (877) 847-4444; fax: (212) 369-8000; <www.hotelfranklin.com>.* The old-fashioned exterior of the Franklin doesn't prepare you for the attractive modern rooms inside. Though not large, all the modern details have been well thought out, and the human scale of the place and the hotel's friendly staff are definite pluses. Convenient to the subway and Fifth Avenue museums. 47 rooms.

The Surrey $$$$ *20 E. 76th Street (at Madison Avenue), tel: (212) 288-3700 or (800) 637-8483; fax: (212) 628-1549; <www.mesuite.com>.* This smartly traditional hotel offers large rooms with kitchens and pull-out sofas in case there are extra guests. Convenient to Fifth Avenue museums and Madison Avenue boutiques, the Surrey is elegant without being stuffy. The convenient Café Boulud is downstairs. 263 rooms.

THE UPPER WEST SIDE

Hotel Beacon $$ *2130 Broadway (at 75th Street), NYC 10024, tel: (212) 787-1100; fax: (212) 724-0839; <www.beaconhotel.com>.* An apartment building on the way to being a hotel. The good news for travelers is that a cramped New York apartment makes a spacious hotel room, and every room has two double beds and fully equipped kitchenettes. Convenient to the Natural History Museum and Central Park. 207 rooms.

The Mayflower Hotel on the Park $$$ *15 Central Park West (around West 61st and 62nd streets), NYC 10023, tel: (212) 265-0060 or (800) 223-4164; fax: (212) 265-2026; <www.mayflowerhotel.com>.* An old-world original, the Mayflower has spacious, traditionally decorated rooms. Some bathrooms are still being modernized, but the rest of the hotel has been completely renovated to a good standard. The location, near Columbus Circle and Central Park, is convenient, but you'll pay more for accommodation with a park view. 365 rooms

Recommended Restaurants

There are over 10,000 restaurants in Manhattan alone. Many of them are very good, many not terribly expensive. There's no way to give even a small sampling of all of the wonderful options available, so the places below have been chosen because they offer good value for the price (whatever that may be). The restaurants are grouped geographically between Midtown (34th–59th streets), Downtown (below 23rd Street), the Upper East Side (above 59th Street), and the Upper West Side (above 59th Street).

The price categories are based on the average cost of a three-course meal for one, not including drinks or tip. If a higher-priced restaurant offers a fixed-price menu (usually served up to 7pm), you can often save money. All restaurants take major credit cards except where noted.

$	below $25
$$	$25–$35
$$$	$35–$50
$$$$	$50–$75

MIDTOWN

An American Place $$$–$$$$ *565 Lexington Avenue (at 50th in the Hotel Benjamin), tel: (212) 888-5650.* Larry Forgione's interpretations of American regional specialties served in a space graced by Frank Lloyd Wright-inspired chandeliers. Only American ingredients are featured, and the same goes for the wines. The heavenly pot-roasted short ribs of beef are excellent, and the fish selections are also good. Dessert classics include James Beard's berry cobbler.

Becco $$–$$$ *356 West 46th Street (8th and 9th avenues), tel: (212) 397-7597.* Come for the delicious pasta at this rustic Theater District favorite that combines reasonable prices and high quality. The two-course fixed-price meal is particularly good value, especially since the pasta is an all-you-can-eat special. The restaurant is busiest during the pre-theater hours, so you may want to reserve a table for after 8pm.

Cabana Carioca $ *123 West 45th Street (6th and 7th avenues), tel: (212) 581-8088.* The popular draw at New York's original Brazilian restaurant is the economical lunch buffet, but dinner includes specialties like *mariscada* (seafood stew) and *feijoada* (black bean stew with pork, beef, and sausage).

Carmine's $$–$$$ *200 West 44th Street (Broadway and 8th Avenue), tel: (212) 221-3800.* The huge portions of hearty Italian food at this Theater District favorite are served family-style, so the prices aren't as high as they seem at first glance. Always mobbed and loud, but consistently churning out massive quantities at all hours, this is a reliable standby eaterie. The no-reservations policy can lead to long waits, however.

Churrascaria Plataforma $$$ *316 West 49th Street (8th and 9th avenues), tel: (212) 245-0505.* All-you-can eat Brazilian *rodízios* (huge meat-heavy buffet) make this one of the most popular and fun places to go when you are in the mood to eat, and eat a lot. Start at the salad bar, but then turn your dish over to begin the parade of skewered meats, and don't stop until you're about to explode. A *caipirinha* cocktail will set your taste buds on the right track.

Fred's at Barney's $$–$$$ *10 East 61st Street (at Madison in Barney's), tel: (212) 833-2200.* You'd never know you were in the basement of a department store but for the lack of windows at this wildly and justifiably popular lunch spot. The antipasto plate is a real charmer, but the Madison Avenue chopped salad with Italian tuna and the more substantial options are also very good. Don't miss dessert. Dinner is also served, but only until 9pm.

Le Bernardin $$$$ *155 West 51st Street, tel: (212) 489-1515.* Arguably the finest restaurant in the city, Le Bernardin serves only seafood. Every item on the fixed-price menu is a winner, from the simplest pan-seared cod to a whole-roasted red snapper for two. Divinely inspired desserts. If you're only planning on one really expensive dinner during your visit, have it here. No lunch Sat–Sun.

Smith and Wollensky $$$$ *797 3rd Avenue (at 49th), tel: (212) 753-1530.* The well-aged steaks served in this male-dominated classic eaterie are consistently and perfectly grilled. The wine list is also great but (sometimes shockingly) expensive. The less expensive grill around the corner on 49th Street is a good alternative for anyone without an expense account.

Shaan of India $$–$$$ *57 West 48th Street (5th and 6th avenues), tel: (212) 977-8400.* A quiet and elegant northern Indian restaurant, Shaan can be quite expensive when you order from the à-la-carte menu, but both the lunch buffet and the pre-theater fixed-price dinner (5.30–7pm) allow you to enjoy the fine cuisine at more down-to-earth prices.

Virgil's Real BBQ $–$$$ *152 West 44th Street (near Broadway), tel: (212) 921-9494.* Something to appeal to nearly all carnivores. The dry-smoked ribs and brisket are good, but the pulled pork is a favorite. Share the 'pig out' platter to get a taste of everything, and have cobbler for dessert.

DOWNTOWN

Blue Water Grill $$$ *31 Union Square West (at 16th), tel: (212) 675-9500.* Housed in a spacious former bank, this popular Union Square seafood restaurant is consistently crowded. The raw offerings are especially good. The prices are on the high side of moderate but still quite reasonable. Reservations are necessary unless you want to sit outside.

Bolo $$–$$$ *23 East 22nd Street, tel: (212) 228-2200.* Popular American chef Bobby Flay tries his hands at contemporary Spanish cuisine and the results are fabulous. Try the curried shellfish, the roasted lambshank with orso, or the risotto with pine nuts and rabbit. The atmosphere is graceful, with fountains highlighting a long, loft-style room. The crowd is hip and stylish, but if there's a huge wait for a table, you can opt to eat at the bar instead. The menu changes on a seasonal basis, which ensures the freshest ingredients.

Cafeteria $$ *119 7th Avenue (at 17th), tel: (212) 414-1717.* One of Chelsea's trendy and busy options, Cafeteria is open 24 hours and offers reconstructed bistro and diner food for hip club-goers (where else will you be able to get pancakes or grilled salmon at 4.30am?) Consistently good, if not overly exciting.

Cucina di Pesce $ *87 East 4th Street (near 2nd Avenue), tel: (212) 260-6800.* This busy East Village Italian favorite is nothing fancy, but with virtually every main course under $10, what else could you ask for? Pastas and fish are all good. Free mussels for those waiting at the bar. Cash only.

Cucina Stagniole $ *275 Bleecker Street (6th and 7th avenues), tel: (212) 924-2707.* Crowds line up for inexpensive, homey Italian food. There are no surprises on the menu; it's the usual chicken and veal dishes and pastas. The salad is big enough to be shared, and the strawberry antipasto is a specialty.

Dojo $ *26 St. Mark's Place (2nd and 3rd avenues), tel: (212) 674-9821.* The operative word at this East Village hangout is 'cheap.' This perennially popular Japanese diner is one of the busiest places in the area. Breakfasts, particularly the pancakes, are stellar, but the soy burgers and fried chicken are also good. Dojo West (a much nicer room, marginally higher prices) is at 14 West 4th Street (at Mercer). Opens at 11am. Cash or travelers' checks only.

East of Eighth $$ *254 West 23rd Street (near 8th Avenue), tel: (212) 352-0075.* One of the most consistently good (and crowded) restaurants in Chelsea, East of Eighth offers pasta, pizza, and other Italian-inspired fare at moderate prices. The pre-theater menu is a real bargain, especially when you purchase discount movie tickets for the Clearview cinema next door.

Gotham Bar and Grill $$$$ *12 East 12th Street (5th Avenue and University), tel: (212) 620-4020.* This large, airy space is usually filled with well-dressed downtowners who appreciate the exquisite (and very tall) food and well-chosen but expensive wines. Few other upscale restaurants are as inviting to single diners, who can order and eat at the bar in comfort and style. The $20 fixed-price lunch is a satisfying option.

Hangawi $$ *12 East 32nd Street (5th and Madison avenues), tel: (212) 213-0077.* Diners at this vegetarian Korean restaurant will quickly become suffused with a Zen-like calm. Discard your cares (and your shoes) at the door, and try mountain-root vegetables, porridges, and other delicacies you've never heard of before.

Iso $$–$$$ *175 2nd Avenue (at 11th), tel: (212) 777-0361.* The sushi for two at this popular East Village spot is almost larger than the table and well worth the price. Order à la carte if you have your own favorites.

John's Pizzeria $ *278 Bleecker Street (6th and 7th avenues), tel: (212) 243-1680.* The motto at John's is 'No Slices.' And you'll be happy you didn't limit yourself when you order one of the delicious pizza pies, with their slightly coal-blackened, not-too-thick crusts. This is the original eatery, but there's a Midtown location at 260 West 44th Street (Broadway and 8th Avenue). Cash only.

L'Ecole $$ *462 Broadway (at Grand), tel: (212) 219-3300.* A firm favorite because of its moderate prices, carefully composed wine list (among the most reasonable in town), and consistently good French food. Operated as a training center for the French Culinary Institute, its shaky service can be easily forgiven when the check arrives. Where else can you get five (yes, five) courses for just $35?

Nobu $$$$ *105 Hudson Street (at Franklin), tel: (212) 219-0500.* Still wildly popular and trendy (forget Saturday night), Nobu continues to pack in crowds with its innovative nouvelle Japanese menu. Next Door Nobu offers a slightly less expensive menu and a no-reservations policy (for those who won't be dining with Robert De Niro), as long as you don't mind standing in line and being perceived as a nobody, which is anathema to many New Yorkers.

Nyonya $ *194 Grand Street (at Mulberry), tel: (212) 334-3669.* The place to go for an introduction to the delicious (and sometimes spicy) cuisine of Malaysia. The Hainanese chicken is good, but don't overlook spicy beef *rendang* or one of the equally tasty seafood dishes.

Patría $$$$ *250 Park Avenue S. (at 22nd), tel: (212) 777-6211.* The fiery and tangy *ceviches* and *empanadas* are specialties here, but everything on this South American menu is delicious. The emphasis is on seafood. The room, light and airy during lunch, buzzes at night when all is plunged into semi-darkness.

Second Avenue Deli $ *156 2nd Avenue (at 10th), tel: (212) 677-0606.* The harried and sometimes cranky staff add to the mystique at this classic East Village Jewish deli. Come for the corned beef, and you'll never be let down. Don't be put off by the crowds swarming around the counter, as many are just waiting for a take-out to carry home.

Shabu-Tatsu $ *216 East 10th Street, tel: (212) 477-2972.* At this small, popular Japanese restaurant, diners choose a selection of thinly sliced meats and vegetables for *shabu-shabu* (swirled in a hot pot of seasoned water), *sukiyaki* (a Japanese stew), or *yakiniku* (cooked on a grill) and cook it themselves in the middle of the table. There's a second location of Sabu-Tatsu at 1414 York Avenue (at 75th Street).

Shanghai Cuisine $–$$ *89 Bayard Street (at Mulberry), tel: (212) 732-8988.* Shanghai cuisine is more than just soup and dumplings, as this Chinatown spot proves. Fresh interpretations of traditional specialties, including smoked fish and mock duck, will reward the adventurous.

Union Pacific $$$$ *111 East 22nd Street (between Park and Lexington), tel: (212) 995-8500.* The serene setting – the spacious rooms are set apart from the dark entrance by a quiet wall of water – and fine Asian-accented food paired with an extensive selection of wines (with a tilt toward Germany and Austria) make for a fine evening. The tuna tartare is excellent. Service is solicitous without being overbearing.

Union Square Café $$$$ *21 East 16th Street (near Union Square), tel: (212) 243-4020.* Gracious service and reliably good food are two reasons this is one of New York's perennially favorite restaurants. Although the Mediterranean-inspired cuisine is no longer cutting-edge, the food still dazzles in unexpected ways. Even the fried calamari, now a restaurant staple, is heads above the chewy appetizer most people have come to expect. The extensive and reasonably priced wine list is an added bonus.

Red $$ *19 Fulton Street (at Front), tel: (212) 571-5900.* In the culinary wasteland of the South Street Seaport, this southwestern spot is at least attractive and fun. The food is reasonably good and not as overpriced as most of the other choices in the area, so grab a margarita and relax.

THE UPPER EAST SIDE

Café Boulud $$$$ *20 East 76th Street (near Madison, in the Surrey Hotel), tel: (212) 772-2600.* Daniel Boulud (owner of two 4-star restaurants in New York City) has also mastered the art of casual elegance. Calling this a tarted-up bistro (which is what it is) strikes a note of sacrilege, but the label certainly can't detract from what a great chef can do when he takes his gloves off.

Pamir $$ *1437 Second Avenue (74th and 75th streets), tel: (212) 734-3791.* This place serves some of the best Afghan cuisine in New York. There's also a branch in Midtown, on First Avenue at 58th Street. Pamir is a good place to go with a group of friends, so you can all sample and share different dishes.

Pastrami Queen $ *1269 Lexington Avenue (85th and 86th streets), tel: (212) 828-0007.* This is the best bet for a good, reasonably priced meal near the Upper East Side museums. The mild pastrami, which melts in your mouth, can be ordered in a towering sandwich or on a platter big enough for two. Other deli meats are equally delicious, but the cooked dishes tend to be merely okay, and are more expensive.

Sarabeth's $–$$ *1295 Madison Avenue (at East 92nd Street), tel: (212) 410-7335.* Bright, cheery and incredibly popular, Sarabeth's is best for its home-style breakfasts and brunch. There are two other locations, one at 423 Amsterdam Avenue between 80th and 81st streets, tel: (212) 496-6280, and another in the Whitney Museum at 1295 Madison Avenue at 75th Street, tel: (212) 410-7335.

THE UPPER WEST SIDE

Lemongrass Grill $$ *2534 Broadway (between 94th and 95th streets), tel: (212) 666-0888.* This reasonably priced Thai chain can be found all over the city. Good bets are lemongrass pork chops (diners share them), spring rolls, and pad Thai. Other locations of the Lemongrass Grill are on 34th Street (between 3rd and Lexington avenues), 80 University Place (at 11th Street), and 53rd Avenue A (4th Street).

Shun Lee $$$ *43 West 65th Street (Columbus Avenue and Central Park West), tel: (212) 595-8896.* Those used to take-out noodles, fried rice, and General Tso's chicken will be amazed at how refined Chinese food can be. Attached to the original restaurant is the much less expensive Shun Lee Café, and on the east side is Shun Lee Palace (155 East 55th Street between Lexington and 3rd avenues, tel: 212/371-8844).

Tavern on the Green $$$ *67th Street (at Central Park West), tel: (212) 873-3200.* An enormous *faux* palace sprawled among the greenery of Central Park, the Tavern on the Green is better known for its landmark status and dizzying bustle of waiters serving over a hundred tables than it is for its menu. That said, the mostly American specialties have improved over the years, and the indoor/outdoor atmosphere cannot be matched. Reservations recommended.

INDEX

The world's largest collection of visual travel guides

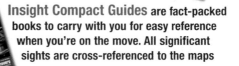

Insight Guides provide the complete picture, with expert cultural background, remarkable photography and full coverage of sights and attractions

Insight Pocket Guides highlight an author's personal recommendations for the best things to see and do on a short visit. They include a large fold-out map

Insight Compact Guides are fact-packed books to carry with you for easy reference when you're on the move. All significant sights are cross-referenced to the maps

Berlitz Pocket Guides put the world in your pocket with detailed information, an easy-to-use A–Z of practical advice, eye-catching photography and clear maps

(Apa Publications)